DREAM CARS

GALLERY BOOKS
An imprint of W.H. Smith Publishers Inc.
112 Madison Avenue
New York, New York 10016

A Bison Book

DREAM CARS

Richard Nichols

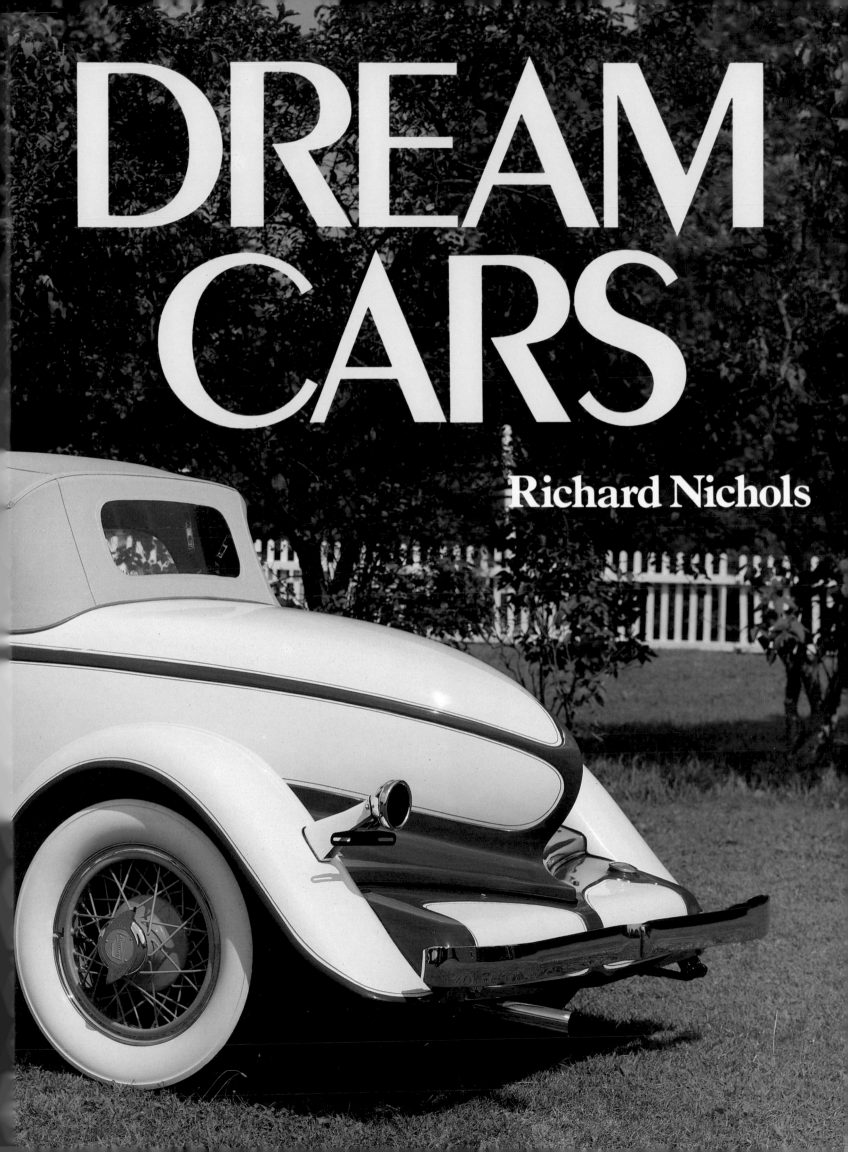

Published by
Gallery Books
A Division of W.H. Smith Publishers Inc.
112 Madison Avenue
New York, New York 10016

Produced by
Bison Books Corp.
15 Sherwood Place,
Greenwich, CT. 06830

ISBN 0-8317-2428-5

Printed in Hong Kong

3 4 5 6 7 8 9 10

Page 1: The dream car of Texan Carroll Hall Shelby, the
Cobra matched the best of British – a body by AC Cars – with
Ford's all-American V8 engine.

Pages 2-3: The unmistakeable lines of the Auburn Speedster
epitomise the style of American sportsters of the thirties.

This page: Forerunner of the formidable range of Porsche
road and race cars that continued successfully into the
eighties, this is the 356A from 1958.

Contents

Introduction

Mass production was invented by Henry Ford simply as a means to an end; ignoring the resulting increase in his personal fortunes, it was to attain the ideal of making so many cars so cheaply that everybody could have one. It was a goal later seized upon by his ardent admirer Adolf Hitler when he persuaded, cajoled and bullied those around him into making the 'people car' a four-wheel reality and a world best-seller, a goal which has long been the objective of just about every major auto maker in history. Even now there are vast industrial combines all over the world who are dedicated to making you the proud owner of a new car at a price you can afford.

Human nature, however, is nothing if not perverse, and having passed reasonably swiftly from being priced out of the market to being priced slap in the middle of it, the bulk of the car-buying population obstinately continue to aspire to something they can never own on the grounds of immense cost. Fortunately there are one or two people left who can afford the ultimate road-

Above: Mercedes' 6.25-liter Type K established a reputation as the fastest touring car in existence in 1926.

going motor car, the most expensive race car, the most historic piece of nostalgia, and the supercar's existence is assured by the same means that the great cars of the past continue to be maintained and restored. For the true enthusiast and for the idle rich, the pursuit of automotive excellence has no financial limit.

Within the auto industry the term 'dream car' is accepted as meaning those cars which the design studios have created as representing future ideals, future possibilities or even future impossibilities. But

there seems to be no valid reason why only the privileged few should be entitled to dream about the sort of car they would like to build. Most of us, it should be said, enjoy similar dreams, although they are usually confined to cars which already exist.

For those of us who will never be able to afford a coffin-nose Cord, a Ferrari GTO or a brand new Rolls-Royce Corniche convertible those cars will remain confined to our dreams.

Richard Nichols

Robert Bamford and Lionel Martin finished their first car at their Kensington, London, factory in 1913. It had a 1400cc Coventry Simplex engine in an Isotta-Fraschini chassis, a top speed of about 70mph and was intended to be a competitor to the successful Bugattis. Robert Bamford retired after World War I had intervened and Lionel Martin assumed sole control of the company that bore their names, although he needed extra financing from Count Zborowski. From then on the specter of financial collapse would haunt activities, with frequent changes of control and ownership typical rather than unusual.

The new name was chosen after Lionel Martin had reviewed the names of all the birds, flowers, fish and animals he could think of; eventually he got round to place names and added his surname to the Aston Clinton hillclimb venue where he had experienced some considerable success, and Aston Martin was born. Taken over after near collapse by a syndicate including ace mechanic Augustus Bertelli, Aston Martin had considerable race success including a class win at Le Mans in 1932, but at the end of the year was acquired by R G Sutherland. He kept race involvement and success high, and continued to develop new models; under him designer Claud Hill produced a prototype road car called the Atom in early 1939.

After the end of World War II the company was again in financial difficulties; industrialist David

Brown bought it after he saw an advert in *The Times* offering a sportscar company for sale. Months later he also bought Lagonda, founded in 1898 by Wilbur Gunn when he built his first motorcycle and named after Lagonda Creek in Springfield, Ohio. Progressing from motorcycles to cars, Lagonda established themselves as makers of innovative, high-performance vehicles, including the 1937 V12 and a postwar 2.6-liter with the dual overhead-camshaft (ohc) engine designed by W O Bentley.

After coming under the control of 'D B', as he was known, both marques were assembled in Hanworth from engines made in Yorkshire and bodies by Mulliners at Birmingham. Then David Brown bought

Above: By 1963 the DB5 was offered as a convertible, and with an automatic transmission option for the first time. The engine (*inset left*) had grown to four liters and 280hp.

Tickfords at Newport Pagnell, where Ian Boswell had been building car bodies in the factory which had housed Salmon & Sons, coachmakers to the nobility since 1820. They had made fabric bodies for cars up until the outbreak of World War II in 1939, and Boswell had taken over in 1945.

It was from here that the DB series, a combination of the Atom and Lagonda's postwar 2.6-liter engine, began, although the true merging of the different makes only occurred with the 1950 DB2. And as the DB series developed on the road Aston Martin continued with race involvement, quick to put the lessons of the track on to the street, and were the first to develop a disc-brake system for the road. But the race-track was abandoned in 1963, the year that saw the arrival of the DB5.

By now the engine had grown through 3.6 to 4 liters, producing in excess of 280hp, and the DB5 was offered as a convertible and with an automatic gearbox option. Always expensive, Aston Martin were edging into the supercar league, and confirmation of this arrived from the unlikeliest of sources. The books of Ian Fleming had translated well on to the screen, and James Bond – played by Sean Connery with his tongue planted firmly in his cheek – was little short of a national hero. Gadgetry had already featured heavily in the Bond films and the fast car was an essential part of his equipment, but in *Goldfinger* the producers went totally overboard. The DB5 featured in the film was the single most famous car Aston Martin have ever made, probably one of the most famous *anyone* has ever built.

Rotating licence plates, hydraulic rams, onboard radio direction finding, machine guns built into the front fenders, bulletproof screen in the rear deck and a facility to eject nails or oil and lay a smokescreen were

Left and below left: Even Aston Martins come in for conversion sometimes. Purists will have their own opinions about this DB5 shooting brake.

Above and below: The Aston Martin Lagonda, with squarish good looks, powerful V8 engine and the most sophisticated electronic dashboard in the world today.

all built in, but it was the ejector seat – which disposed of unwanted passengers – that captured most people's imagination.

As is customary in film production there wasn't just one car; Aston Martin built four, two for use in the film and two replicas for publicity purposes. All were sold when filming of the second Bond epic in which they featured, *Thunderball*, was finished, although one had been stripped of the extras and returned to stock DB5 specification. When the new owner of this car discovered its history he went to the expense of restoring it to its former configuration before selling it on. When

last heard of this car, like its three counterparts, was in a private collection in the United States.

David Brown sold Aston Martin in 1971 and the company changed hands again in 1974, when it seemed for a while that closure might be inevitable. It was under the control of Peter Sprague and George Minden (who subsequently sold their interest) that Aston, now well and truly established as makers of supercars, produced the two cars which have remained as the pinnacle of the firm's development. The first evidence of this made its debut at the Earl's Court Motor Show of 1976, when the futuristic Aston Martin Lagonda stole the show.

Styled by William Towns, the Lagonda was long, low and wide, featuring the wedge shape which has been the vogue among car stylists for some while. The engine was the 5.3-liter four-camshaft V8 which has no quoted power output but probably delivers between 400 and 450hp. Whatever the truth, it pushes the big 4500lb Lagonda to over 140mph with no apparent effort and can sustain it all day.

Extensive use of high-technology electronics and fiber optics was well ahead of its time in 1976 and, although initially troublesome, has now set a standard of control and instrumentation for others to follow. The dashboard is blank until the key is turned, and then lights up a digital display which covers every single function from speed, trip mileage and inside and outside temperature to battery voltage. As a complement to this array are no less than 20 touch-sensitive switches which control all the car's functions from high beam to bi-level airconditioning. The dash is burr walnut, the trim is leather and the carpet Wilton; *Motor Sport* magazine called it 'staggeringly opulent,' as any car with a £65,000 pricetag should be.

Left: The wildly expensive Bulldog. Aston Martin don't list it in their catalog, but say they would build to order if asked.

Right: Gullwing doors and a mid-mounted V8 were part of the Bulldog's impressive specification.

Below left: With a height of only 43 inches, passenger access to the Bulldog was far from easy – even with those doors.
Far left: engine detail
Below right: Concealed lighting doesn't pop up – instead, the Bulldog's hood drops down.

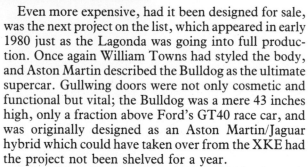

Even more expensive, had it been designed for sale, was the next project on the list, which appeared in early 1980 just as the Lagonda was going into full production. Once again William Towns had styled the body, and Aston Martin described the Bulldog as the ultimate supercar. Gullwing doors were not only cosmetic and functional but vital; the Bulldog was a mere 43 inches high, only a fraction above Ford's GT40 race car, and was originally designed as an Aston Martin/Jaguar hybrid which could have taken over from the XKE had the project not been shelved for a year.

Instrumentation was once again digital, airconditioning was fitted, and the Connolly leather trim was as usual applied around burr walnut dash and Wilton carpets. Despite the burden of this heavy load the Bulldog had an estimated top speed of around 190mph, although the basic 5.3-liter powerplant common to the other AML cars was mounted amidships. The extra speed came from a 60 percent power increase which lifted the output to over 600hp, thanks to dual Garrett AiResearch turbos.

Typically, the Bulldog featured independent front suspension and de Dion rear axle, the latter an unusual configuration in a mid-engine car. And, unusual for an AML road car, steering was unassisted rack and pinion for better feel. Built as one-off testbed, the Bulldog was not designed to go into production, although AML said they would sell it 'if the price was right.' Since there are no plans for a second Bulldog the 'right' price is likely to be astronomical.

Auburn-Cord-Duesenberg

Erret Lobban Cord began his career in the auto industry as a repairer of Model T Fords, a business which met with mixed fortunes. He was said to have become a millionaire three times before he reached 21 – and lost his millions every time. At 30 years of age, and now with lasting wealth, he joined the failing Auburn company as general manager, bought a share in the firm and proceeded to put it back on the path to financial security and strength.

Aside from being – fairly obviously – a clever engineer himself, Cord could also spot talent in others, and employed Gordon Buehrig, Harry Miller and Count Alexis de Sakhnoffsky soon after he became President of the company in 1926. Almost in the same breath he bought control of the Lycoming engine plant and the Duesenberg company.

The Duesenberg brothers, Fred and August, had begun by making bicycles in their adopted home town of Des Moines, Iowa, before going into motor racing after building their first car in 1903. The Duesenberg company was formed in 1912 to build race cars, and their success led inevitably to the manufacture of road cars. The first was the Model A tourer of 1920. Duesenberg road cars were heavily based on the knowledge and expertise gained from racing and were excellent examples of advanced engineering. They soon established the same superb reputation as the race cars had garnered on the track, where they had collected an assortment of speed records and race wins, taking Indianapolis in 1924, 1925 and 1927.

Cord's tough leadership and empire-building ambitions had brought a vital and effective combine into being, and Auburn-Cord-Duesenberg proceeded to flourish in no uncertain terms. Unfortunately Cord's timing was particularly bad, and all of his projects reached fruition in the same fateful year – 1929. Miller patented his version of front-wheel drive – a technique first demonstrated by Walter Christie in 1904 – in 1929, the same year in which the first car to bear the Cord nameplate, the L29, appeared. Designed by Carl van Ranst, it carried Miller's front-drive setup (which utilized a de Dion front axle on four quarter-elliptic springs), but nostalgia makes it look rather better now than it did at the time; good-looking it may have been, but it was also heavy and rather ponderous, and not the car with which to enter the Depression years and emerge unscathed.

Meanwhile Count de Sakhnoffsky had designed the body for the Auburn Speedster, a two-seat, high-speed car which, like other cars of the time, was sold with a

Right: Probably the most familiar and well-known example of the ACD products was the 851 Speedster, this one dating from 1935.

Below: With less elegant but equally dramatic styling, this 1931 model is the 8-98-A Auburn Speedster.

Left: Cord began to produce cars in his own name and introduced a number of styling changes like the horizontal radiator grille.

Above: Rare as a hardtop, this is a futuristic 1936 model.

Below left: By the late thirties the 'coffin-nose' Cord, with its retractable headlamps, was a good-looking car on its way to almost legendary status.

Below: The 1937 Cord 812 supercharged Phaeton.

cost a great deal less than did its major rival, the Stutz. This may account for the survival of the ACD empire over the next few awful years; the bubble burst one morning in 1929 when the selling on Wall Street began, and no manufacturer emerged from the Crash unscathed. Some didn't emerge at all.

But the wily Cord had spread his net fairly well, and covered most eventualities. Concentrating on the Auburn Speedster, he had left the other part of the group to get on with their own business, giving the Duesenberg brothers a blank check to fund the construction of the fastest car available to the American buyer. Fred was an exceedingly fine engineer but August, widely known as Augie, was an excellent designer, and the result of Cord's desire was the superb Duesenberg Model J.

Again powered by a Lycoming-built straight eight, with dual overhead cams and four valves per cylinder, it delivered 265hp and had a top speed of 116mph as a two-seat tourer. Even with full sedan coachwork, some of which rivaled the best that Rolls-Royce America was producing from Springfield, the Model J could turn in a top speed in the 100mph-plus bracket, and fulfilled in every way the brief which Cord had laid down for it. The Model J featured chassis lubrication by an onboard oil pump, plus dashboard warning lights for oil and battery levels. Supplied without coachwork, the Model J was sold all over the world wherever there was anyone wealthy enough to pay more than $8500 for a car with no body at a time when the most prestigious Packard came complete for less than $6000. Once again, though, the timing was unlucky and the Model J appeared for the first time in the fateful year of 1929.

guarantee that each car had been individually tested at 100mph. The power for this record-setter was supplied by a straight-eight Lycoming engine mated to a well-tried and proven Duesenberg supercharger, although it was also available without the blower. With it, 'Mormon Meteor' Ab Jenkins broke records when he maintained the speedster at 100mph for 12 continuous hours on the Bonneville salt flats.

This was an exceedingly elegant motorcar, greeted with instant delight from all who saw it, and remains today a full-fendered classic which is typical of the grace, elegance and excess of the late twenties. Also it

It was with this lineup that ACD survived the Crash and entered the years of the Great Depression. Overall the early thirties saw production in the US auto industry cut by 50 percent and more, although output had been re-established by about 1935. Erret Cord directed his energies, and those of the ACD empire, wholeheartedly into rebuilding; at one end of the scale he was fortunate in that although the Crash erased a great many small fortunes, those who had been very rich before it were either still very rich or just plain rich; and even before the Crash you had to be very rich to afford a Duesenberg.

Capitalizing on the fact that one part of his empire at least still had just as many clients, the Model J was superseded by the outstanding SJ, a supercharged design reckoned to be good for about 130mph; the price was also measured in big numbers, and a chassis with engine was about $15,000. On top of this some of the leading coachbuilders of the day – Murphy, Le Baron and Derham – built some of the most classically elegant car bodies ever seen. Clients were frequently royalty of some sort, many of whom were displaced and with few outward signs or symbols of past status available; ex-pensive cars were a reliable method of establishing a level of personal worth and wealth. There were even a few members of the new Hollywood star system who could afford this sort of car, and Clark Gable was one of Duesenberg's SJ owners.

Following this example of the best the ACD empire could offer was a car which actually surpassed it, if anything could be said to have done so. The Cord 810 was the ACD masterpiece, their pinnacle of excellence. Although it was by no means as attractive as the Auburn Speedster or the beautiful SJ Duesenberg, the 810 'coffin nose' was still a superbly good-looking car. Styled by Gordon Buehrig, its lines were less flowing than its stablemates but still clean and balanced. The traditional upright radiator shell was gone, replaced by wraparound horizontal gills, and not even the huge convoluted chrome headers which snaked out from the sides of the hood could detract from the lean economy of its styling. In large part this streamlined front was due to clever adaptation of aircraft landing lights, providing the coffin nose with retractable lamps buried in the front fenders – still a rare (and expensive) feature on cars 50 years later.

Right: The 1929 Duesenberg tourer showed that the brothers were capable of building for more than simply speed.

Below: Now at the Auburn-Cord-Duesenberg Museum, the beautiful SJ Roadster was – and is – one of the most elegant of the thirties' sportsters.

The 810 also offered the combination of front drive and independent front suspension for the first time ever on any car, although this, combined with the powerful Duesenberg-supercharged engine, led to pronounced wear in the hub bearings. Production problems – especially with the transmission, which featured a mixture of electromagnetic and vacuum-operated gear-change – meant that the 810 was never built in large numbers, and very few genuine examples survive today. All the ACD marques have become much prized by collectors and museums worldwide.

Having weathered the Depression, the ACD combine finally failed in 1937; Fred Duesenberg died after a crash in 1932 and Augie made an abortive and unsuccessful attempt to revive the Duesenberg operation in 1947. Cord still had the Lycoming plant, though, and it continued to prosper, especially as a supplier of aero engines between 1939 and 1945. ACD reappeared briefly in the seventies, selling fiberglass boat-tail Auburn Speedsters using original factory drawings but based on a Lincoln chassis and a 427 Ford V8, but even that enterprise vanished without trace after the death of Erret Cord in 1974.

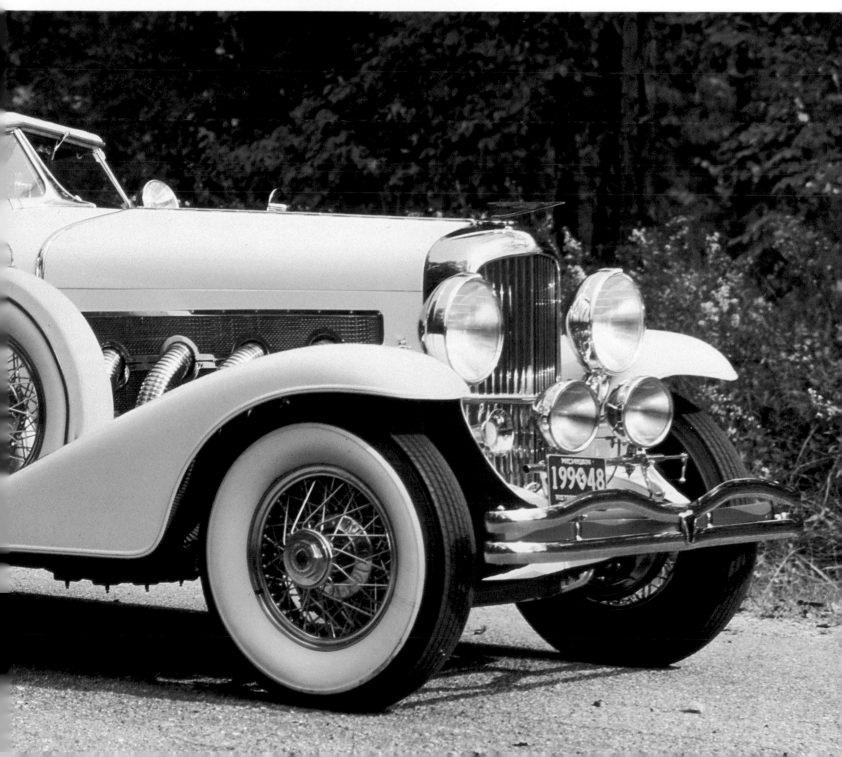

Bentley

Walter Owen Bentley was widely known to his friends and associates simply as 'W O'. A railway apprentice with an enthusiasm for the motorcar, he won a London-to-Edinburgh reliability trial in 1907 and decided that he would form a company to build his own. In partnership with his brother, 'H M', he began by importing various French makes – La Licorne, DFF and Buchet – and continued racing, in a DFF. He had commenced several record-breaking attempts which had to be curtailed at the outbreak of World War I.

After the war, W O formed the Bentley Car Company and more or less carried on his prewar activities, with a primary interest in motor racing. It was an interest that would bring the Bentley name to the forefront of the motorsport world as the marque estab-

lished a supremacy which would last almost a decade. It was a lone Bentley which represented Britain at the very first Le Mans and it was Bentley who went on to imprint their name indelibly in the history of this most famous motor race in the world, winning it five times in seven years.

It was this short 'golden age' which made Bentley a famous name though precious little money, and the company was extensively backed by the cash of the Hon Dorothy Paget – inspired principally by patriotism – and of Captain Woolf 'Babe' Barnato, who

Below: The imposing 1927 Bentley 4.5-liter configured as a four-seat open tourer. The Bentley badge (*inset bottom*) is from a 1930 Speed Six.

took an exceedingly active role in the racing activities, winning the Le Mans race three times.

The 24 Hours was inspired by the French Grand Prix – which was held at the Sarthe circuit – and the 1922 Bol d'Or 24-hours event, and was the work of the Automobile Club de l'Ouest (who are still the organizers), a journalist and the Paris representative of Rudge-Whitworth, makers of motorcycles and wire wheels. The first event was thus the Rudge-Whitworth Cup. Some 30 of the 33 starters finished the event, which W O had at first ridiculed; he said that no car would last the 24 hours and at first refused to have anything to do with it. But he was talked round, and a private entrant – John Duff – took the Bentley name to Le Mans and one of W O's new 3-liter cars came in fifth, after being out of the running for more than two hours while a leaking petrol tank was mended. The team of John Duff and Frank Clement had broken the lap record three times, though, and made a fairly strong impression – even on W O himself, who had spent the whole 24 hours working in the pits.

Armed now with brakes on all four wheels rather than just the rear pair, the same car was back in 1924 as the only British entry in a 40-car field; this time it emerged the winner, setting the standard for a period of racing dominated entirely by W O's 'Bentley Boys'.

This was pure *Boys' Own* stuff, with a cast of characters straight out of a Dornford Yates novel performing the heroics. 'Babe' Barnato shared his drive with Sir Henry 'Tim' Birkin, and the rest of the Boys were jockey George Duller, theatrical impresario Jack Dundee, Doctor (of medicine) Benjafield and journalist 'Sammy' Davis.

The next two years were a thin time for the Bentley Boys, and Lorraine Dietrich took the honors in 1925 and 1926. But in 1927 the team was back at Le Mans,

the three-liter supplemented by the big 4.5-liter. In a six-car accident at White House corner the 4.5-liter was wrecked and put out of the race. The three-liter of Dr Benjafield and Sammy Davis (the latter at the wheel) was extricated from the wreckage and, despite being fairly severely damaged, drove on to win.

In 1928 the 4.5-liter showed its class and scored a third win at Le Mans for W O's Boys, but that was a mere curtain-raiser for the main event. In 1929 the Boys were back at Sarthe, with a new car. There had been a 6.5-liter touring Bentley since 1925, a car of impressive dimensions and appearance, and for the 1929 event this straight-six engine was placed into a

Above: The 4.5-liter from 1928 differs from the '29 (right) in detail, although both are bodied by Roger Cook.

Below: Cockpit detail from the 1928 car; note the hand throttle and ignition advance/retard control on the steering-wheel hub, and the chassis number on the dashboard.

Right: Built in 1929, this 4.5-liter 4-seat tourer was bodied by Vanden Plas.

Left: In its most romantic form, this is the 4.5-liter 'Blower' Bentley. The supercharger is crank-driven and carried ahead of the engine (*below left*) rather than belt-driven and mounted above it. The dashboard layout (*below*) is rather more complex than the touring models.

convertible sportscar of equally majestic proportions. The Bentley Speed Six was quite simply the stuff of which legend was made and was entrusted to Babe Barnato, the rest of the team being equipped with 4.5-liter cars.

The huge Bentleys rumbled through the night and into the following day with a clear lead; it was the big six of Tim Birkin and Babe Barnato which clinched victory for W O, but the rest of his Boys simply added to their growing charisma as their cars came home in second, third and fourth places. Later the same year Bentleys triumphed at the first 500-mile endurance race at Brooklands; Jack Barclay and Frank Clement were first in a 4.5-liter, Sammy Davis and Jack Dundee established the fastest lap – 126mph – and brought their Speed Six home in second place.

In 1930 the Boys were back at Le Mans, with the challenge this year coming mainly from the seven-liter Mercedes of Caracciola and company. The Boys pulled it off again, though, and Barnato took his third successive Le Mans flag.

But the era was drawing to a close. The replacement for the Speed Six was destined to be a vast eight-liter affair of some 220hp, and it was launched just in time to encounter the worst effects of the Depression and bring the company to its knees. In 1931 the company went into receivership, and it seemed as if the long-absent

All pictures: Built in 1930, the squat shape of the Speed Six is unmistakable and perhaps even more attractive than the open tourers. Once owned by Bentley director Woolf Barnato, this is the famous 'Blue Train' car.

All pictures: The Bentley Mulsanne Turbo. After only 12 years during which production reached only 4000 vehicles before being taken over by Rolls-Royce, Bentley acquired a reputation built exclusively around fast tourers based on the hugely successful Le Mans cars. Now the Mulsanne, distinguished by its body-color radiator shell, upholds the company tradition once more.

Napier concern might buy Bentley up and come back into the industry when they offered the Receiver £103,000. But the eight-liter Bentley was a good car, and could quite easily have sold well if it went into production. Had it done so, it would have been competing in the very expensive, prestige end of the market. In the event, Rolls-Royce bought Bentley for £125,265 and used it as a badge for their own designs, slightly cheaper than Rolls-Royce. The partnership was acrimonious to say the least, and W O went on to do his best work for Lagonda, not Bentley.

In recent years Rolls-Royce have used Bentley as an almost experimental base for turbocharging; a Camargue body with an anonymous body-color radiator shell denotes the Bentley Mulsanne Turbo, launched at Geneva in 1982 – the first Bentley to have had any personality of its own since the thirties with the sole exception of the R-Type Continental. With the Garrett AiResearch blowing through a four-barrel Solex carb, placed in a sealed plenum chamber in the center of the vee, the 2½-ton Mulsanne slots 0-60 in 7.4 seconds, 0-100 in 18 and tops out at 135mph, making it the fastest car Rolls-Royce have ever made.

Although they never give horsepower figures away, the Mulsanne is guessed at around 300, and gets its rapid acceleration from the Rolls system which eliminates lag by keeping the turbo spinning all the time. Like the rest of the Rolls-Royce production items it is expensive – and if you have to ask the price

BMW M1

Originally makers of aircraft and aircraft engines, BMW was formed from the merger of two separate companies to meet the demand for airplanes occasioned by World War I. Their first car was, strangely, an Austin Seven built under license in Germany as the Dixi by Fahrzeugfabrik Eisenach, incorporated into BMW in the early twenties. From this they progressed to sports touring cars and developed a fine reputation.

At the end of World War II the partition of Germany left them starting virtually from scratch and they produced some odd vehicles until Paul Hahnemann set them back to work building a new four-door sporting sedan with a lightweight four-cylinder ohc engine. From then on the company had continued as a leader in this field, with Alex von Falkenhausen's super-efficient engines a major factor.

Using motorsport as a sales tool is commonplace for the industry, and BMW have been no exception. With a model range exclusively of fast tourers, the company obviously appeared in relevant races and during the sixties and early seventies featured heavily in the European Touring Car Championship. While continually demanding and competitive, this kind of racing is far from glamorous, and to most people German cars in racing meant only one thing – an endless procession of Porsches. The Group 5 BMW CSL

developed around 1000hp in turbo form but was less reliable than without it; although they kept Porsche on their toes they still couldn't break the hold of the smaller cars. Clearly BMW needed a smaller and lighter vehicle of their own, a two-seat wedge which would allow that 1000hp to be used.

They had, in 1972, shown such a car around Europe; a bright orange mid-engined gullwing which had never been intended for production. However, it provided a platform, a base to work from, and around this was designed the M (for Motorsport) 1. In order to qualify for Group 5 racing – and the M1 was never intended to be anything more than a completely shameless homologation exercise – 400 of the cars had to be built, and this in itself created problems. They had to be built in two versions; a road car had to be available since there was no chance that race requirements would use 400 units and less chance that a road car would need the full 1000hp.

Built on a spaceframe chassis, the body was styled by Ital design in fiberglass, with conventional doors, and the driver sat well forward, ahead of the 3423cc straight-six engine which had four valves per cylinder in an alloy head. Road cars had chain-driven overhead camshafts and timed injection, delivering 280hp at 6500 rpm, which was enough to give a 0-60mph time of

All pictures: BMW's abortive attempt to go racing resulted in the extraordinarily good-looking – and fast – M1 sportscar, of which a total of only 449 examples were ever built.

5.4 seconds, 0-125 in 20.9 seconds and a top speed of 160mph. The road car was quite simply a detuned racer, something which BMW made no attempt to hide – in fact the sales brochure went to considerable pains to point it out. The main difference between road and track powerplants was that the race engine featured gear-drive to the cams and slide-throttle injection. Dry-sump lubrication was common to road and race cars, as were four-wheel ventilated disks, rack-and-pinion steering and four-wheel independent coil-and-wishbone suspension, while a ZF five-speed gearbox was chosen. This box appears in large numbers of supercars from different makers, generally because it's the only one which can handle the huge power outputs – in this case a rewarding 470hp at 9000rpm without the benefit of turbocharging.

But the BMW factory was by no means geared to the production of low-volume cars, still less the handbuilt care which would have to go into anything as finely tuned and balanced as the M1. So they looked around for someone to build it for them. The search led, not unnaturally, to Italy, where the construction of such cars is relatively commonplace. Eventually a deal was struck with Feruccio Lamborghini's underworked factory, badly hit by the recession.

That this was a mistake soon became apparent. Lamborghini's cash shortage was so acute that subcontractors and suppliers were witholding vital materials and parts, afraid that they would never be paid. Without them Lamborghini were stuck in the vicious circle which precedes collapse, unable to build the cars and thus unable to get the money to pay their suppliers. They went bust in 1978, two years after the M1 project had got under way, and having built precious few prototypes. Without the 400 production models needed to qualify for Group 5 BMW were now stuck with a handful of exceedingly expensive cars, and in order to satisfy management they had to come up with something to justify their existence.

The solution they arrived at was the Procar series, which was designed by BMW and FOCA (Formula One Constructors' Association), originally to put the top five Formula One qualifiers into a 24-car grid composed entirely of M1s immediately prior to each of the F1 Grands Prix. Drivers' sponsorship contracts put paid to that idea, but a way round it was eventually found at great cost and the series went ahead. Six of the 470hp cars were built by BMW themselves at Munich, and the rest of the 24-car grid was built by Osella of Italy and Project Four in Britain.

It was an eight-round series and winners included Elio de Angelis, Nelson Piquet, Jacques Lafitte, Hans Stuck and eventual series winner Niki Lauda. And production of the road cars was now in the hands of coachbuilders Baur, who were making them at a very slow rate. So slow, in fact, that by 1980 there were still nowhere near the 400 needed for homologation into Group 5, leaving BMW to sponsor yet another expensive 'stopgap' Procar series, which was a close-fought battle between Alan Jones and Nelson Piquet.

It was the last year that the Procars were fielded. BMW were in any case turning towards straight Formula One involvement, and even though they eventually made a total of 399 road cars and 50 race cars, they never really launched their planned assault on Group 5. Some were built in Switzerland by Peter Sauber and did quite well – an M1 won the Nurburgring 1000kms in 1981 – but the intention to put the 1000hp turbo Group 5 cars into contention came to nothing. But in private hands the race cars have done rather better and lasted somewhat longer – an M1 took Class B at the 1984 Le Mans 24 Hours.

The road cars continue to be esteemed collectors' items – as would almost anything which was limited to a numbered build of 399 units – although not purely for their rarity. Like other BMW products the M1 is an excellent piece of machinery – and even though it is a detuned racer it makes none of the compromises which owners of, say, roadgoing GT40s or Lola T70s are forced to live with. Although the cockpit is small it is not cramped, but like many mid-engined two-seaters legroom for the six-foot-and-over driver is negligible. The interior trim and dash covering are far from spartan, although the instrumentation, with 170mph speedo and tachometer running up to the 9000rpm racing maximum, is totally functional. So also are the standard electric windows, airconditioning and radio, although they too are unusual features on a race-bred car like this.

And yet despite its civility, despite the tractability which allows it to pull smoothly and cleanly at town pace, it is a race car and will jump from standstill to 125mph in 21 seconds. It will cruise quietly and effortlessly at 120mph all day, and will consistently do so at a much lower level of overall engine noise than is common to mid-engine cars, especially the really fast ones.

The M1 continues to be raced successfully and continues as a highly desirable road car, although rarity and price ensure that it will remain nothing but a dream for all but 449 people.

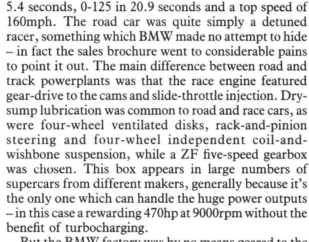

Bugatti

Italian-born Ettore Bugatti had his first personal encounter with a petrol-engined tricycle in 1898; within a year the Milanese machine-shop apprentice had built his own tricycle with which he achieved a superb record in local races of eight wins from ten events. Thus encouraged, he moved from Italy to the De Dietrich company, based in German-held Alsace, and practically without a pause began to build cars under his own name. A Bugatti finished second in the 1911 French Grand Prix, and the same run of success continued after the end of the war in 1918.

In the period between the wars the racing Bugattis were practically invincible; the car which led to this domination was the Brescia, named after the racetrack at which it took the first four places in the Italian Voiturette Grand Prix of 1922. This was basically a prewar Type 13, but the four-cylinder 1368cc engine, with its single overhead camshaft, was replaced by the larger straight eight, which was based on Bugatti's experience building aero engines for Duesenberg during the war years. Such was the domination of this car that it won over 1000 events in the period of one year, 1925-26, and a further 800 in 1927, as well as scoring five successive victories in the Targa Florio.

The race-car chassis was known as the Full Brescia, but there were longer touring chassis as well, known as Brescias Modifiés; off the track the Bugatti name was by now associated with fast, luxurious tourers with a distinctly rakish appearance, low-slung swooping bodies crouched behind the famous Bugatti grille. This latter may have been simply based on a horseshoe, but it was also the same shape as the entrance arch to the Bugatti premises at Molsheim; it's impossible to say which came first.

Perhaps Bugatti may have continued to make the same sort of race and sports car forever, but during that first decade of peace there came a string of luxurious sedans and closed tourers which are widely considered to be among the best of their kind ever made. Certainly not cheap, they became almost exclusively the transport

The Bugatti Brescia, named after the race in which it was so successful, was manufactured in two versions – the Brescia Type 23 4-seat tourer, or Modifié (*above*), and the short-wheelbase Full Brescia (*left*).

of the exceedingly wealthy and were reputedly inspired by the visit to Bugatti of a wealthy English lady. She had complimented *Le Patron* on his racing and touring cars, but rather acidly observed that anyone wanting a motor car of great distinction must necessarily speak with Rolls-Royce.

This conversation is reputed to have taken place over the dinner table which Bugatti promptly left, heading directly to his drawing board to rectify the situation. The result was one of the most desirable cars ever built, the two-ton, 20-foot Bugatti Royale.

It appeared first in 1929, powered by a massive 12.7-liter straight-engine capable of hurling the huge car up to a maximum speed of 125mph at a time when the first short link in the Italian *autostrada* had been completed in 1923 and was still the only piece of freeway anywhere in Europe. The German *autobahn* network wasn't started until 1935, so there was no road anywhere within driving reach where the Royale could approach anything like its maximum speed.

Minor concerns of that nature had little or nothing to do with the Royale's *raison d'être*, however. It had been created simply to put Bugatti on the map as a manufacturer of the very best automobiles available, and had been named appropriately; the next step was to make sure that it retained a suitably high degree of exclusivity. In order to achieve this Bugatti refused to sell the Royale to simply anyone who could afford it, and reversed the traditional routine of car purchase. Instead of prospective buyers examining the car to see if it met their needs and would fulfil their requirements, *Le Patron* scrutinized his prospective clientele to make sure that they came up to the same high standard as his motorcar. Simply having enough cash or a title wasn't good enough.

It was not a technique which encountered overwhelming success, however, and for several years not one Royale was sold. Eventually six were built and four sold, the other two being retained by members of the Bugatti family.

At the same time as he had reversed normal car-buying procedures, Bugatti had turned the tables on the lady who had spoken of Rolls-Royce in such glowing terms. Anyone with enough money could have one of *those*, but only the chosen few were privileged enough to be allowed to buy the incredibly expensive Royale. Understandably very few Royales were ever made, and still fewer survive today. Although practically every car museum has its Bugatti racer, and the Brescias come up in auctions of antique automobiles on a fairly regular basis, the Royale is just as sought after now as it was 50 years ago.

Standard coachwork was a four-door sedan sat behind a tremendously long hood; sweeping fenders, huge lamps and the Bugatti horseshoe topped it off. But the Royale also went to specialist coachbuilders, and the best example of their art is beyond doubt the Weinberger-built drophead model in the Henry Ford Museum at Dearborn; this is not only stupendously good looking, it is also a touch on the expensive side, even for a collectors' item. The Museum recently decided to Americanize their collection and part with the Bugatti, but only at the right price; an offer of $1 million for the car was turned down.

The production life of the Royale was limited, being restricted to the 10 years between its introduction and the outbreak of World War II; it took two years of postwar court hearings for Ettore Bugatti to regain tenancy of his factory, and it was eventually restored to him in 1947. He died in his sleep the same evening, and there were no more Bugattis of any kind.

Both pictures: The fabulous
Bugatti Royale. Only six were
built and four of them sold; the
other two remained within the
Bugatti family.

Cadillac

Henry Ford's second venture into automobile manufacture, the Henry Ford Motor Company, was reorganized after Ford's departure at the end of 1902 following policy disagreements by an engineer who had worked for the Springfield Armory during the Civil War and later for Colt. Alfred Sloan, the man who made Durant's dream for General Motors come true, said of this engineer, 'Quality was his God' – something future customers would not only believe but frequently depend on.

Henry Leland had been technical adviser and engine supplier to Ransom Olds and then a director of the re-formed ex-Ford company, now named Cadillac after the founder of Detroit. The first Cadillac of 1902 was powered by a single-cylinder Ford engine, but Leland presided over much in the way of technical advance, and 12 years later his own V8 engine became the standard Cadillac powerplant.

Cadillac's reputation for excellence was built quickly, and although it was Ford who introduced the auto industry to mass production it was Leland who first began to standardize vehicle components (from one manufacturer) to the point at which they were interchangeable. Cadillac were first with both electric lights and electric starting, and began to rival Packard as the most prestigious American vehicle.

Following the Crash, Cadillac – now minus Leland, who had left to form Lincoln in 1917 – introduced one of the greatest American cars of all time, the V16 Sedan de Ville. The chassis, at 148 inches, was nothing if not luxurious, and the rest of the car followed the same theme. Coachwork on all of them was by Fleetwood, whose work was by now exclusive to Cadillac, and made the most of the flowing grace of the fenders to compensate for what was of necessity a large and squarish body behind a vast, imposing grille. Convertible versions were even better looking.

The engine was one of the better creations in the history of Detroit. Designed by Ernest Seaholm, it was a 45-degree V16 454ci which produced 165hp at only 3400rpm. Aside from the fact that the engine was so low-revving, the quiet smoothness was aided by hydraulic tappets. Two updraft carburetors were located outside the blocks and were exhaust-heated by the dual-header system.

The V16 stayed in production unchanged from 1931 to 1938, during which time a respectable 3863 examples were built. This was no bad record for a pretentious car which was by no means cheap; many of the companies which had survived the Crash were finding the Depression years just as tough, and even those who aimed for the still-wealthy top end of the market were having difficulty. With the security of General Motors around them, Cadillac continued to thrive while the smaller independents went to the wall; in 1938 another V16 engine was introduced.

Unlike the original this was not an overhead valve unit and, although it produced slightly more power from a smaller 431ci, was generally held to be inferior in most respects. It delivered 185hp, featured dual distributors, water pumps and carburetors and had nine main bearings at the heart of the 135-degree block.

Above: Built shortly after the type's introduction in 1932, this Cadillac tourer has the original smooth V16 powerplant.

Below: The V16 was most often built as a formal limousine; the pictured car, from the ACD Museum, dates from 1933.

Only 511 of these cars were built between 1938 and the end of 1940, and a trifling 61 of them were made in that final year before the whole of the US auto industry gave its full attention to the war effort.

By the time the thirties drew to a close the big V16 engine was somewhat dated and the chassis was, by any standards, huge. The trend in the industry was downward in size, both for cars and their engines, and it is doubtful whether the V16 would have lasted very much longer had production not been terminated by the war.

Postwar Cadillacs were still built to the same high standard – their slogan had been 'Standard of the World' since the days of Henry Leland – and were, incredibly, still built on almost the same scale. The Series 75 grew from 136 inches in 1945 to 146 in 1950 and 149 inches in 1954, but that was the Cadillac nine-passenger stretchout for state occasions. The Series 70 Eldorado Brougham, introduced in 1957, began life on a modest 126-inch chassis but in 1959 became the Cadillac Eldorado in three forms, the Seville hardtop

coupé, the Brougham hardtop sedan and the Biarritz convertible coupé, all riding a 130-inch chassis. Cadillac said later that the 1959 Eldorados were the most ostentatious cars they ever made, and while that statement may have been entirely truthful it was still not completely accurate: the 1959 Eldorado was the most ostentatious car *anybody* ever made.

1959 was the year in which almost the entire US auto industry discovered fins and applied them with great enthusiasm to all their products, none more so than Cadillac. The Eldorado had rear fins which were large enough to grant inflight stability to the largest rocket yet launched from Cape Canaveral.

The front aspect was no less dominating, the hood itself a vast area of sheet steel flowing into quad headlamps and a rambling honeycomb grille dominated by a huge chrome bumper. And although the whole Cadillac range featured hi-rise rear fins the Eldorado, as their highest-price model (excluding the monster Series 75 formal limousines), had the biggest. It also featured the high-output version of the standard Cadillac 390ci V8 motor, putting out 345 instead of 325hp.

The air suspension introduced on the Brougham in 1957 had, by means of an air compressor and a piston-operated air 'spring' on each wheel, given Cadillac the first self-leveling air suspension on a passenger car which took in air from outside rather than the closed system which GM had offered on other vehicles. It had not been a marked success, though, mainly because the air reservoirs at each wheel leaked, and many were replaced soon after purchase.

Other standard equipment on the Eldorado was available throughout the whole Cadillac range, and makes impressive reading even now. Cruise control was commonplace and signal-seeking radios were also fitted. Other features which didn't make it into production but which had been tried out on the 1959 Cyclone experimental car (which if anything had bigger fins than the Eldorado) included a sensing system which raised the convertible top and closed the side windows if it began to rain.

The Eldorado was priced according to its immense size and specification. At a time when Lincoln had nothing over $6000 and Chevrolet's typical prices were

Right: Returning to business in the postwar period, Cadillac produced this formal saloon in 1947, with body work by Durham.

Below: The 1957 Eldorado Brougham shows distinct signs of the massive fins which would dominate the '59 models; introduced to Detroit in the early fifties, by Harley Earl, they – and the curved glass areas – signpost his fascination with the jet aircraft of the period.

less than $3000, the Eldorado range began at $7401, again only exceeded by the $10,000 Series 75. But not even the big limo could match the Eldorado Brougham for price – a staggering $13,075. The high price of the Brougham was due entirely to the fact that for 1959 production of this model had been handed over to Pininfarina; the parts were shipped and assembled in Italy, and whole cars were sent back. Because of the way it was done the cost was astronomical; a mere 99 of them were built in 1959, and 101 the following year.

Despite their huge cost, and although hindsight has lent the whole range an elegance and grace which was perhaps not completely evident at the time, the Biarritz Convertible is the most impressive of the three Eldorados. It is the stuff of film and television, it is the huge pink car featured in just about every cartoon series of the late fifties and early sixties, it is the sort of car movie moguls gave to starlets and genuine screen goddesses gave to their friends at Christmas. Paul Getty owned a 1959 Eldorado – but his was, naturally, the Seville hardtop; at no time in its history was the Biarritz a car to be taken seriously.

Chameleon

Mercedes already have a fine reputation as manufacturers of luxury limousines without any help from anyone else, but their already sumptuous machinery is frequently the subject of some even more upmarket trimming and styling modifications by small companies dotted around Europe. This is necessarily an expensive process, often because Mercedes lend little active help to the companies thus engaged, leaving the customizers to buy their cars on the open market themselves or to perform their minor miracles on a vehicle already owned by someone rich enough to require their talents.

In recent years one of the biggest markets for top-of-the-range vehicles treated this way has been the oil-rich Middle East, where the initial $40,000 purchase price of something like the 500SEL is a fraction of many people's incomes or total wealth. One of the companies now heavily involved in this market is the London-based Chameleon Cars, who will do anything to any car for anyone with the money to pay for it but whose specialist activities are based on the Mercedes range.

Typical of this is their Pullman limousine, which starts life as a 500SEL with all the factory options. This is pulled to pieces before being given a 36-inch stretch to allow for two rearward-facing seats or a massive

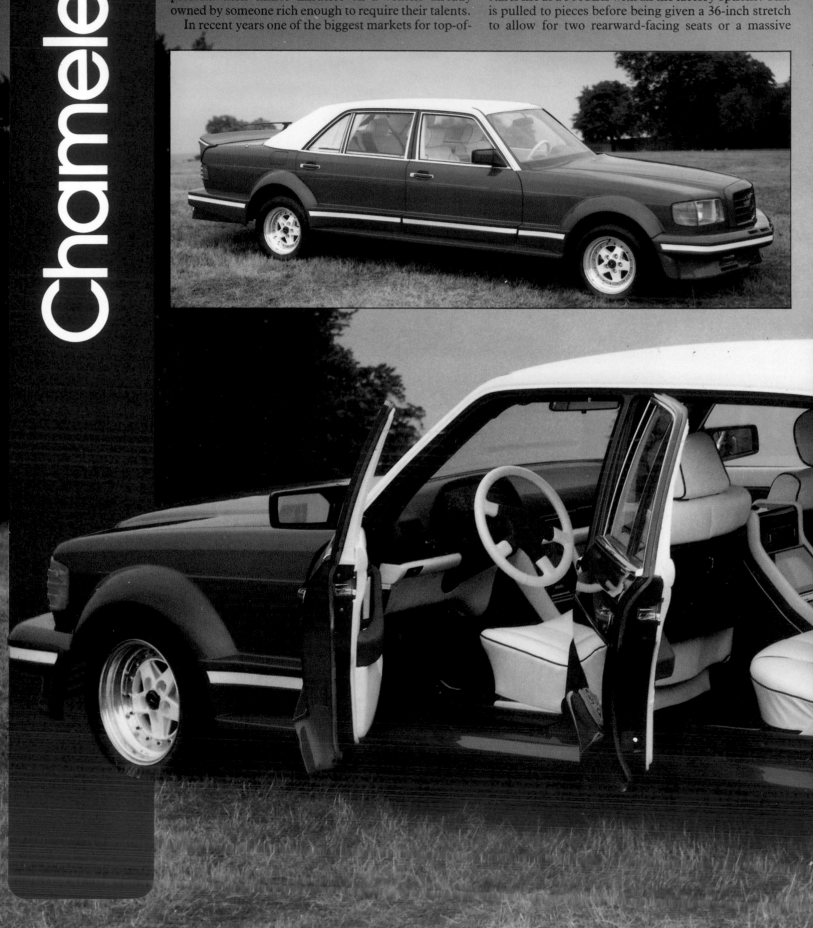

All pictures: One of several companies specializing in bespoke automobiles, Chameleon Cars produced this Tornado conversion of the Mercedes 500SEL.

in-car entertainment console which contains anything the customer requires. Typical specifications include satellite communications, a color TV and video player, rack hifi system, cocktail cabinet, icebox and fold-up picnic tables. The TV, video and hifi systems are often duplicated in the front of the car so that the chauffeur (or the owner, should he deign to drive himself from time to time) can enjoy a different program or type of music from his passengers. Where this option is installed there is generally a glass divider between front and rear; this can either be of the raise-and-lower variety, or for the security-conscious can be permanent and bulletproof, supplemented by an intercom system to link front and rear.

Cocktail cabinets naturally contain crystal decanter and glasses and, like the entire console, may be trimmed either in burr walnut or in the same materials as the rest of the car. Interior trimming costs can put anything up to $50,000 on the price; materials are usually a mixture of Connolly hide, velour, Wilton carpeting and burr walnut. All the door-cappings, for example, are remade in walnut, and Chameleon, like the master coachbuilders of the twenties and thirties, employ skilled cabinet-makers and craftsmen capable of handstitching the interior trims.

Gold plate appears in a number of the specifications, as also do solid gold fittings. Gold accessories, like pens and sunglasses for each passenger, are often included, and an increasing number of cars are being sent out with gold-plated handguns in a concealed compartment next to each seat.

Outside specifications are equally overpowering. Body trim panels in the current style of Cd customs, which include front airdam, wheel-arch extensions, sideskirts and rear-deck spoiler, alter the appearance of the car enormously and are often to individual specifications. They are all made from Kevlar, the space-age fiber which appears on race and rally cars as body and chassis parts; it is lighter and stronger than steel, will not rust and can be built up in layers to a point at which it is no longer simply impact resistant but proof against high-velocity gunfire.

Naturally all these extras make life difficult for the standard mechanical components of the car. In most cases the airconditioning units are uprated for desert application, and in order to deal with this a bigger and more powerful generator/battery combination are fitted. Suspension is uprated to deal with the extra weight, and Chameleon have developed their own supercharger which gives an 85hp bonus to the engine, restoring overall performance to its original level before the extra weight was added.

The blower was originally devised for their Typhoon, which is based on the 500SEC sportscar, since it was felt that although most customers would accept (or perhaps not even notice) the drop in performance in the big fully-loaded sedans, there is no point in owning a sportscar, no matter how opulent, unless you have sportscar performance.

The Typhoon is not stretched like the Pullman, but first steps in its creation are still pulling it apart. Where the Pullman gets Kevlar add-ons and inserts in door

and rear deck, the Typhoon panels are all remade in this virtually indestructible material. Suspension is lowered all round by removing a coil from each spring (which rules out the Mercedes self-leveling suspension option), super-wide Pirelli low-profile tires on Gotti aluminum wheels compensate in the roadholding department, and the Typhoon's interior gains the same sort of luxury trimming as the Pullman.

And although it is a much smaller car, it *does* have two rear seats – so although limited space means there's only room for one video player, there are two color TV sets and the hifi system has two cassette/radio units linked into the bi-level amps, graphic equalizer and six-way speaker system so that back-seat passengers can change the tape or tune the radio without having to lean *too* far forward. Gold fittings or gold plate can be ordered, and gold plate fills in the ducts ahead of the rear wheels; they were originally installed to cool the Typhoon's rear brakes, but were ultimately found to be unnecessary.

Out of the factory the 500SEC costs around $40,000 and tops out at about 140mph. From Chameleon, armed to the teeth with all the luxury there is available, the price of the Typhoon is closer to $150,000. With the ATM blower boosting it to over 300hp, the top speed is slightly higher.

All pictures: The Typhoon is based on the Mercedes 500SEC, for which Chameleon have developed their own supercharger to compensate for weight increases occasioned by the extra bodywork and the many interior additions.

Citroen SM

André Citroen was a French national of Dutch parentage – an engineer who had been a gearmaker to the car industry before the outbreak of World War I and a manufacturer of munitions during it. After the war ended he converted his factory to the manufacture of motorcars, adopting as his emblem the double chevron which was representative of the double helical tooth formation of the gearwheels which had made him a wealthy man.

After a moderately good car, the 10hp, his first big success came with the 5CV – a car of some 7hp, thanks to the difference between metric and imperial horsepower – which was initially a two-seater. With the addition of a centrally-positioned rumble seat it became widely accepted as the 'Cloverleaf'. It was to the French motor industry what the Model T was to the American, the Austin Seven to the British and the Laubfrosch (tree-frog) to the German. In fact the Opel Laubfrosch was a bolt-for-bolt copy of the Citroen and the subject of a successful lawsuit. Adam Opel paid gladly; in fact he had budgeted for it.

Citroen's own prestige as an engineer was high; the company introduced the all-steel body to Europe in 1925, were the first with Ford-derived mass production, and then made the first monocoque car in 1934. Unfortunately the tooling and production costs of the elegantly innovative front-wheel-drive car were too much, and the company had to be rescued by Michelin. André Citroen died shortly afterwards, and never saw his Traction Avant in production.

It was the car the Citroen company had been waiting for, and saw them permanently established as a major force in the European car industry. It continued to be built for the next 23 years, and almost 760,000 of them were made. Few of the prewar roadsters survive today: in fact most of the existing Tractions are the later 1911cc 60hp models with which the model ended its life in 1957.

It was replaced by the revolutionary DS 19, which was the first Citroen with truly revolutionary aerodynamics, giving it a futuristic appearance. It was on this model that first use was made of hydropneumatics;

the DS 19 had a self-leveling suspension system which 'collapsed' when the engine wasn't running, and pumped itself up after the car was started. It was also the jacking system for tire-changing, and gave power to the brakes – inboard front disks were standard.

The original engine was a hemi-head update of the long-stroke inline four which had been at the heart of the Traction, although it was later replaced by a more modern powerplant. Other refinements which came later were the swiveling headlamps, which were also part of the hydro-pneumatic system and turned with the steering wheel, automatic transmission and a five-speed manual stick shift. Total sales of the DS series – 19, 21 and Pallas – ran to 1.5 million until it was finally dropped in 1975.

Although Citroen had never made a real sportscar other than the Traction roadster, they did have ambitious plans for a genuine GT car, and their acquisition of the ailing Maserati setup in 1968 was, from this point of view, extremely fortuitous. Plans for a coproduction between Citroen and Fiat had collapsed after Fiat had

The SM (*Left and above*) was developed during Citroen's brief ownership of Maserati and used an incredibly compact V6 engine.

made it clear that they wished to have control over the product; Citroen would not accept, and the collaboration never really got off the ground.

Work went ahead on the Maserati-based Grand Tourer, which would eventually emerge in 1970 as the Citroen SM. It was destined to put all the technical features of the DS series into a more modern and sophisticated design, with yet more technical advancement. Maserati were called upon to design the engine for it, and the result was a compact and swift, if overcomplex V6 installation based on an existing unit.

The cleverest part was its compactness. A mere 12.25 inches long, it was all-aluminium, with the induction system for the three dual-barrel Weber downdrafts built into the cylinder heads. Quad overhead cams were chain-driven by a convoluted system hidden deep inside the engine. In order to accommodate the front-drive setup the engine was fitted to the car backwards, with the transmission sticking out towards the front, which made any work on normally vulnerable items like timing chains not only time-consuming but also extremely expensive.

To compensate, the engine produced 180hp from its 2670cc, and a healthy 171 ft/pounds of torque at 4000rpm; enough to get its 3000lb kerb weight up to almost 140 mph – not bad for a full four-seat tourer which dealt in ultimate luxury at every level. To be fair, most of its 116-inch wheelbase was full up with engine, since Maserati had chosen to ignore the gearbox-under-engine solution which was then gaining currency on front-drive cars and is now all but universal, so the passenger compartment was by no means kingsize.

Even so, the Citroen SM boasted all the advantages of the DS series and a few more besides. The engine/transmission layout had enabled the SM to inherit inboard front disks, outboard rear disks and the Citroen self-leveling suspension. New power steering – with servo assistance in directly inverse proportion to engine revs – made parking fingerlight but allowed the driver maximum 'feel' at cruising speed. Power centering was also a feature; left untouched, the wheels would return from either lock to straight ahead if the engine was running. In any case the 9.4:1 steering ratio was unusually quick, and one full turn of the wheel would take the wheels from straight ahead to the full lock position in either direction.

Across the front were six lights in two pairs of three, totally enclosed behind a flush glass panel which also included the license plate and gave the SM smooth aerodynamics. There were two long-range driving lamps, two dipped driving lamps and two swiveling lamps which were, like those on the DS, hydraulically powered and swiveled with the steering wheel, advancing a few degrees ahead of the front wheels. Each bank of three lamps was fitted on a pivot through its horizontal plane, and was thus self-leveling. Application of hydraulics here too prevented the lamps swinging wildly, but regardless of load and other factors like heavy braking, the SM's headlamps remained horizontally aligned.

Tinted glass and airconditioning were options and fuel injection was added in 1974, but the oil crisis had arrived and cars like the SM were going out of fashion. Citroen's own finances were pretty shaky as well, and when their Berliet truck operation had been handed on to Renault and Peugeot had reluctantly stepped in to help with car production, the Maserati connection had been acquired by De Tomaso and the SM was gone; some 13,000 of them were made in total, and they remain the subject of owners' clubs and collectors' auctions today.

All pictures: The SM used all of the complicated Citroen hydro-pneumatic systems for suspension and braking, and also added some new ones of its own for headlamp leveling, etc.

The Corvette was introduced in 1953 (far right) as a radical fiberglass sportscar. By 1956 (above) it had changed shape for the first time and grew to real elegance in 1957 (top).

Zora Duntov is frequently referred to as the father of the Corvette. He is frequently – and mistakenly – credited with the design of the car as well, but didn't in fact join General Motors until May 1953, five months after the car had first been shown as a concept at the New York Autorama and a scant month before Job One rolled off the production line at Flint, Michigan.

Duntov did go on to have a great deal to do with the Corvette, though, and was responsible for much of the all-important development work. Initially the Corvette was powered by an extremely ancient and outdated engine, the stovebolt six, designed in 1929. Development for Chevrolet's first V8 engine in decades was already happening when Duntov came to GM, but it was he who made it the legendary powerplant it has since become.

Planned to combat the supremacy of Ford's very old (1932) flathead, the V8 was a natural choice for the Corvette, and when Duntov gave it first a wild camshaft of startling duration and effect and later pushed the fuel-injection system into production the by-then 283-inch smallblock produced 283hp, reckoned at the time to be an ideal ratio of power to capacity. The hot-rodders had adopted the smallblock almost immediately it appeared, and Duntov's work – especially that camshaft, which became an almost mandatory performance option – confirmed their choice. The engine went on to become the most widely-produced powerplant ever, and more than 35 million have since been made. Since its introduction in 1955 its capacity has been standardized at 350ci and it has become the accepted GM powerplant for passenger vehicles.

Duntov's first task had been to give Corvette some proper suspension and steering geometry, improving its handling almost beyond recognition. Even so, the improved version was hardly a raging success. GM production philosophy was not, in the fifties or since, geared to low-volume specialist vehicles and the Corvette received less than total backing from the corporate structure. Had Ford not produced the Thunderbird two-seater when they did the Corvette may never have made it past 1955. Later, its reputation as America's only real sportscar took a sound beating

from the Cobras of Carroll Shelby and might have suffered further at the hands of his Mustangs had not the fuel crises of the time shut down the Ford Total Performance Program.

Even the Corvette's independent rear end was bought by compromise, and the transverse-leaf spring was part and parcel of careful budgeting, as were the front suspension components, stolen straight from the existing Chevrolet lines. The introduction of disk brakes was delayed more as a result of perfectionism than accounting, though, and a whole generation of Corvette owners is now familiar with the incredible straight-line stopping power of the vehicle's massive four-wheel disks.

Probably the only person to give the Corvette sound backing at boardroom level outside of those initially concerned with its creation was the energetic and enigmatic John De Lorean, who turned the production line and quality control on its head at the same time as he upped the sticker price to make low-volume production more financially reasonable. Part of that same program meant the delaying of production-line changes which were in hand, and partly accounts for the fact that the Corvette retained one body style virtually unchanged for 15 years.

Although there wasn't a lot wrong with the style itself, 15 years is an exceptionally long time in the auto industry. That fact hadn't escaped attention at General

Above: The 1968 Corvette, styled by Larry Shinoda under Bill Mitchell's direction and the ultimate visual expression of the sportscar's characteristics.

By 1976 the Corvette had grown a plastic nosecone and tail section (*top left*) and by 1979 (*top*) the glassback style introduced for the Silver Anniversary 1978 model (*left*) had replaced the 'sugar-scoop' rear. By 1981 (*above*) the Corvette was long overdue for its restyle, and the changes were mere cosmetics like spoilers and pinstripes.

Motors and the absence of revamps was certainly not due to a lack of ideas or enthusiasm. Indeed, it was during that period that many of the most exciting Corvette development prototypes were built. The mid-engined prototypes never saw production, however, even though they looked as good and handled as well as a great deal of European sporting machinery.

What *did* happen was that Bill Mitchell's Sting Ray race car was popped into production as the 1963 Sting Ray, and all the really advanced work which had been going on behind the scenes was relegated to the realms of the purely experimental. And although Corvette engineering was somewhat hamstrung by all this, insofar as it was never as advanced as the design team wished, it was far from being bad. The order forms were never short of option boxes, either, although they were almost exclusively concerned with engineering hardparts rather than cosmetics. Other car buyers could have stripes, wheels, wings, whatever – with the Corvette the emphasis was on final drive ratios, spring rates and engine parts, something totally in keeping with the ethos and also an underlining of the basic truth that it was a very good-looking car anyway.

All pictures: The new Corvette was shown in 1983, introduced that fall and designated a 1984 model. The 1985 car, shown here, features the same styling and electronic dashboard. Its major change for the model year was the scrapping of the 'crossfire' throttle body fuel injection in favor of a more conventional setup.

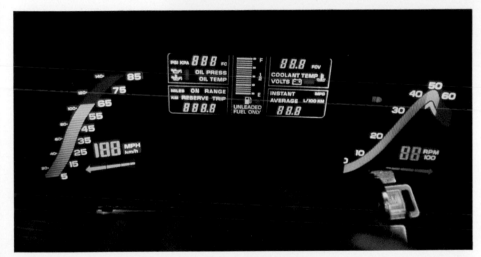

But there were a number of aftermarket bits available, and the height of fashion in 1963 was a one-piece rear window kit which modern Corvette enthusiasts quite properly regard as being not very short of vandalism. In any case the split-window Sting Ray was only in production for a year and is rare enough without the help of the customizing brigade.

Much the same happened in the Jubilee year of 1978, when the sugar-scoop rear window treatment was dropped for a one-piece glassback. There were aftermarket kits immediately available which converted it to a liftback, although anyone doing that to an Anniversary model is unlikely to be popular within 500 miles of Bowling Green, Kentucky. There were plans for a factory liftback, but sealing problems – which afflicted the aftermarket kits – and tooling costs delayed its introduction for a year. Very shortly afterwards, the factory supplied Corvettes as stock with the airdam and rear spoiler which was also becoming vogue-ish with the bolt-on boys.

In general the Corvette, particularly the post-1963 shapes, can only be harmed by alteration and the introduction of body-color wraparounds front and rear made that even more true. Corvette station-wagons, four-wheel-drive Corvettes and the airshocks-and-sidepipe variety are consequently, and happily, still reasonably rare.

There are one or two people, like Frank Milne and Art Richards, who have been repaneling Corvettes for some while; in the main their work has been tasteful, although still unlikely to win friends among the ranks of the purists. About the only acceptable Corvette body modifications are those from Eckler, and a full set of Eckler parts will double the price of a Corvette if not its resale value. Everything except the T-tops gets changed, and although it does make an essentially sleek shape somewhat fatter the Eckler cars have a certain brutish elegance all their own.

The arrival of the all-new for 1984 shape seems to have put a stop to all this, though. Apart from being priced clean out of the accessory market anyway, there seem to be few beneficial changes which can be made to the flatter aspects of the new body. That said, the current crop of race Corvettes do display a lower airdam, some side skirting and a somewhat promiscuous fender flare...

De Tomaso

Allesandro De Tomaso took up motor racing in his native Argentina in 1951, but by 1959 had moved to Italy and rather cheekily set up shop in Modena to build his own single-seaters while he was still working as a mechanic for Maserati. He formed De Tomaso Automobili in 1960, and his first cars under that name were based on the Oscas he had been racing; soon they became De Tomaso-Fords at the beginning of what was to be a long association with the Ford Motor Company. These latter cars were entered in Formula One during the 1970 season, and De Tomaso works drivers included such luminaries as Tim Schenken, Brian Redman and Piers Courage. Still the team fared badly,

and were withdrawn from racing halfway through the season. Away from Formula One, De Tomaso sportscars enjoyed a more encouraging run of luck, and though he occasionally became involved with other European makers for short periods De Tomaso always came back to Ford as a source for his engines.

He had been lucky with sportscars powered by small British Ford engines. His first commercial project had been the Vallelunga, powered by the 1500cc Cortina engine and with a fiberglass body styled by Ghia; as with Ford, De Tomaso would remain loyal to Ghia, eventually buying the company completely as the De Tomaso cars built a reputation for themselves. In fact

De Tomaso himself had an acquisitive nature, and during a short period bought Benelli, Moto Guzzi, Vignale and Maserati, saving the latter from extinction in 1976 and subsequently inspiring production of the four-seat Kyalami.

But the De Tomaso Vallelunga was built only in small numbers: probably less than 100, although there are no production records to prove even this figure. But the next project was already in the pipeline, and the Mangusta was scheduled to make its debut at the 1966 Turin Motor Show. Power was again from Ford, but this time De Tomaso looked to the bigger American V8 engines to give his car the sort of power which the

Below: The Mangusta was the first result of the Ford/De Tomaso collaboration, using the Ford V8 engine and a Giugiaro-styled body.

factory a few miles up the road was currently getting from their engines.

The same formula had already worked for Ford once; their 289ci V8 engine, settled into a chassis from the small independent AC factory in England, mixed with some Shelby racetrack genius, was proving to be a highly potent, almost lethal combination called Cobra. There seemed no reason at all why the combination of ex-race driver, small chassis builder and Ford V8 shouldn't work again, and the result of the co-operation between the companies would be sold by Ford's Lincoln-Mercury Division in the United States and called – Mongoose.

The Italian name is far better known, however, and the prototype which appeared at Turin in 1966 bore a 500hp De Tomaso-built all-aluminum version of the 302ci Windsor engine in a 43-inch tall fiberglass body styled by Giugiaro (still at Ghia) and was called Mangusta. The prototype from Turin finally made production with a midmounted Ford-built 289ci iron motor and with a steel-and-aluminum body. It was fast enough though, with a usable 270hp from the Ford engine, and went into immediate but not especially rapid production. Just 401 Mangustas were built in five years (making it now an exceedingly rare vehicle), but mass production was never the De Tomaso strongpoint. Like many other cars from race and sportscar builders there were a number of minor changes made and few of the cars produced exactly match the makers' original specification.

While this may have been frustrating for Ford there were still advantages; European sportscars, especially Italian ones, were still very fashionable in the tremendously large – and growing – American enthusiast market. Moreover, the De Tomaso purchase of Ghia had brought this famous styling house, with all its reputation and expertise, within Ford's grasp. Thus there were a number of reasons why Ford should continue their association with De Tomaso, and when the prototype Pantera was drawn up by Tom Tjaarda it too was incorporated into the transatlantic deal and eventually replaced the Mangusta in 1971.

Design and development were all done in Italy, and Ghia produced another low, aerodynamic and eye-catching two-seat body to go over the spaceframe chassis and midmounted engine. The engine was the 351ci Ford smallblock, which was rated at 300hp as fitted to the Torino, but which for De Tomaso produced 330hp. Installed in the Pantera it gave a 0-100mph time of 17 seconds, ran the standing quarter in 14.5 seconds and topped out at about 130mph. In European specification, without emission control gear, the Pantera had a top speed closer to 160mph.

But like the Mangusta before it, the Pantera was not entirely without its problems. Its sales appeal was strong, since it offered all the traditional Italian virtues of design and handling coupled with a high-performance engine which didn't have to be shipped back to Italy every time it needed servicing. Theoretically any Ford garage should have been capable of maintaining a Pantera, but that wasn't always the case. Most of the final refinements which go into a new car before it eventually goes into production are skipped by small specialist builders, otherwise their cars simply wouldn't get built, and De Tomaso seem to have been especially bad at this.

Once again Ford's patience proved equal to the task, however, and they supplied expertise and knowledge which straightened out the production of the car inside two years. In fact the later Panteras, from 1973 onwards, were so much improved that they were specially

All pictures: Held in awe by enthusiasts largely because of its Italian heritage and mid-engined layout, the Pantera, dramatic and brutal, was perhaps the De Tomaso zenith.

Left: The original Pantera, with reasonably clean lines, was followed by the Pantera GTS (*above and below*), once memorably described by *Car and Driver* magazine as 'the disco Countach.'

much closer to the real facts; by 1973 or 1974 De Tomaso's interests had moved away from his road cars and gone back to his first love – racing. He was now deeply involved with Group 3 and 4 racers, and claiming some 570hp from his Ford V8 engines. Attractive as that might once have been for Ford, the climate in America had switched away from performance, and involvement with desperately powerful race cars was by no means as desirable as it had been when the Pantera project had begun. In fact, involvement with very fast sportscars was a great deal less desirable than it had been in 1970 as well, so Ford terminated the relationship – and when they left Modena Ghia went with them.

De Tomaso continued on his way, buying up Maserati and then Innocenti, created two more cars under his own name, the Deauville and the convertible Longchamps, and continues to make Panteras in haphazard fashion. Once again there are no production records, so it's not possible to say how many have been made over the years. In any case there have been several versions since the Pantera L, and it is now also available as the GTS and the GT5. But over the years the cars seem to have been little more than rich men's toys, apparently doing little for De Tomaso himself other than satisfy the occasional passing whim; they have probably achieved precisely the same for those few who have owned them.

In the early eighties came the news that Chrysler boss Lee Iacocca, who was Dearborn's top man during the original Ford/De Tomaso alliance, was to give the Italian firm more than two million dollars of MoPar money to design and build a new Pantera-type sportscar to be sold across America in Chrysler and Maserati dealerships. The engine is likely to be based on the 2.2-liter turbo unit currently powering the Varde Charger under the Chrysler race program, into which Iacocca has already incorporated another racetrack pal from the old days, Carroll Shelby. Perhaps with the old team back together the De Tomaso name can produce enough cars to allow ordinary mortals a chance to grab some of the magic.

designated Pantera L. But Ford had carried out work which should never have been forced upon them; the wipers were totally inadequate for a car with this speed capability but De Tomaso himself was disinterested, saying that the car shouldn't be driven in the rain. And as Federal safety regulations began to affect more than just engine emissions De Tomaso again showed his complete lack of concern; he wasn't interested in bumper height regulations because his car had been designed to be driven, not parked.

This might at first seem to be characteristic of a rather splendid arrogance such as might be expected from a slightly rebellious genius, and that may indeed be the truth. But Ford saw it as a sign of a careless attitude which included half-finished projects and rapidly changing enthusiasms. The latter was probably

Ferrari

All pictures: The Daytona is widely held to be the most attractive and desirable of the modern Ferraris, with simple, classically elegant lines combined with the Ferrari magic. Available as a closed coupé (*left*) and in open, spyder, form (*top*), it makes a worthy successor to the formidable GTO.

There is probably only one individual in the history of the auto industry whose name is better known than that of Enzo Ferrari – Henry Ford. But Ford's name and story are taught in schools and are the kind of thing children are made to learn because it's educational and therefore good for them. They learn Ferrari's name later, of their own free will, right after they see their first car with the prancing horse on the hood.

Il Commendatore skipped school and all formal education to work on automobiles, first being refused a job by Fiat and then campaigning Alfa Romeo race cars under the Scuderia Ferrari banner from 1929 onwards. It wasn't until 1946 that he began to manufacture cars in his own name, and – at first – these were sports racing cars, beginning with a series of 1500cc single-seaters which marked the start of a successful and historic association between Enzo Ferrari and Grand Prix racing.

Ferrari also campaigned road racers in events like the Mille Miglia and Targa Florio, usually with such minimal bodywork as was needed to make them eligible. The 166 series, introduced in 1948, was replaced by a front engined, 3-liter V12 which was the beginning of the 250 series, a car so successful and popular that it is truly the beginning of the Ferrari legend. Up until the 250 he was an Italian manufacturer of reasonably successful race cars, but from then on he

Left: The 365 Berlinetta Boxer is styled in what has become the mandatory form for the modern high-performance sportscar.

was a builder of supercars which were as fast off the track as they were on it.

The 250 Testa Rossa was the most successful of the series, carrying the Ferrari banner from 1958 to 1962, and was the basis for the elegant Pininfarina coachwork which characterized the whole roadgoing series and culminated in the superb Le Mans-winning 250 GTO. While all the 250-series vehicles, whether road or race cars, are clearly identifiable as such, the GTO is the one car in the range which has captured the imagination of enthusiasts and has since become the most sought-after Ferrari ever made.

It was preceded by the 250 GT, a far sleeker and, in absolute terms, better-looking car altogether. The 250 LM was better looking still, certainly to modern eyes, with a shorter and lower hood, driver seated well forward and an engine tucked away in the trunk; this mid-engine configuration which dictates the styling of sports coupés has been proven to give more satisfactory performance and is an industry standard. The long hood, with the cockpit a long way rearward and a cut-off tail, is very much the favored styling of the fifties and sixties.

In fact the 250 series had first appeared in roadgoing form as the 1953 Europa, followed by the sleek Pininfarina 250 GT in 1956. Development work on the GTO had begun at the end of the fifties, and the car was first shown to the Press in 1962 at one of Enzo Ferrari's traditional conferences.

Rather than a refinement of the series, the GTO was the final development, the ultimate which could be brought out of the chassis/engine combination, and it looked the part. For those who preferred their motoring with a little more compromise Ferrari built the 250 GTL (for luxury) and the 250 GTS California, representing the ultimate refinement of the 250 series; the part of the brute was left to the GTO.

Ferrari continued to make some superb GT cars for road use even though the team retired from sportscar racing in order to concentrate on Formula One. The 365 series appeared in 1967, and the luxury of its appointments demonstrated that Ferrari was looking towards the American market as a major source of export sales. It was a 2+2 powered by a 4.4-liter V12 engine of some 352hp, and was fitted with power steering and airconditioning among other little luxuries unusual in racebred vehicles.

But even as the 365 was introduced there was a mounting excitement about a car which was as yet still in development and which didn't appear until the Paris Salon the following year. It was christened Daytona before it had made its appearance and the name has stayed with the type ever since. When it was shown for the first time there was no doubt that it more than fulfilled the expectations of all those who had been waiting for it.

Although modern design practice was heading towards the mid-engine layout, the 365 GTB/4 had its V12 mounted resolutely at the front. However Pininfarina's lightweight styling turned the necessarily long hood into an advantage, making it part of a long slow curve through slim screen pillars and an almost invisible rear pillar to a curved cutoff. If the styling was dramatic the performance was likewise, lifting the car to a 174mph maximum speed and making it one of the fastest road cars ever made.

It was replaced in 1973 by what was, by then, a more conventional mid-engine car, the 365 GT/BB, still using a 12-cylinder dohc engine but this time a 4.4-liter flat, Boxer, version; the other B in the car's designation defines it as a Berlinetta. Performance for this car was

as shattering as that of the Daytona, giving it too a top speed marginally less than 180mph. Styling was again by Pininfarina and it is this shape, similar to that now found in the current Ferrari production models, which is established as the shape for high-performance sportscars of the future; yet again, Ferrari had set the standard for everyone else to follow.

In 1976 the 365 was replaced by a larger-engined version of the same thing. Rated at 4.9 liters, it was given the designation 512BB, and is regarded by many as the best vehicle in production anywhere in the world. All that, though, seemed likely to change with the introduction of the 308-based GTO, a 600hp 189mph twin-turbo monster which is the fastest car ever to come out of Maranello. Also in 1985 the last roadgoing V12 was replaced by the Boxer 12, powering the newest Ferrari of them all, nostalgically to be christened the Testa Rossa.

It's often said that if you want to be a really experienced motorist you should own at least one Ferrari in your lifetime; if that's true, then take your choice from either of the two latest scorchers. Prices begin at a cool $80,000.

All pictures: The 512BB has become accepted as the sportscar par excellence since its introduction in 1976. Fast and elegant, it epitomised perfectly the entire uncompromising performance ethos.

1984 saw the introduction of two new Ferrari show cars which went into production for the '85 model year. Seen here as display models, they reintroduced two legendary names: the Testa Rossa (*above and right*) and the GTO (*below and far right*).

Ford Model T Speedster

General Motors was the combination of several small motor manufacturers welded by the dream of one man and brought to financial stability and success by another. It is the largest motor manufacturing company in the world. But there never was a man called General Motors. Its closest rival was a product of one man's genius, a man who gave America left-hand drive, introduced mass-production, established an eight-hour day for his workforce and guaranteed their wages, who said his love affair with the motorcar began the day he fell off a horse, whose first mass-produced car was only surpassed in the history of volume production by a car founded on copycat precepts and using modern manufacturing techniques, and who gave the world the expression 'any color you like as long as it's black.'

Henry Ford was born at Dearborn, near Detroit, in 1863, built his own quadricycle in 1896 and became manager of the Detroit Automobile Company three years later. When he left, Henry Leland renamed the company after the founder of Detroit, and Cadillac soon became an industry leader.

The Henry Ford Company failed in 1903 and the

Ford Motor Company as we know it today was born. Models A, B and C sold well, the Model N gave Ford security as it sold 10,000 models and after its success Henry Ford dreamed of building a lightweight, 20hp, four-cylinder car capable of carrying five passengers in comfort and to be built in such numbers and at such low cost that everyone would have a car; a Ford car.

In 1908 Ford unveiled his Model T. It was a four-cylinder, 20hp four-seater with a top speed of 40mph and was priced at $850. Ford's previous arguments with his partners had always revolved around the price

Below: With a reputation established building the mass-produced Model T, special order bodies for the Speedster combined with the famous Frontenac engine (hence 'Fronty' Ford) to produce a race car of singular character.

of the product; right from the start he had realized that a small profit on each car, giving it a low selling price, would boost sales to the point at which many small profits would be even better than a few big ones. His beliefs proved to be absolutely correct, and the Model T sold 17,000 units in its first year of production. Only four short years later, production had risen to an incredible 170,000.

And as production volume increased the price went down, encouraging more people to buy, allowing the price to be reduced yet again ... By 1916 the cost was down to $360 and in 1923 the car hit its lowest ever sticker price: $260.

But although the Model T set new standards it also borrowed some old ones (like the Lanchester flywheel magneto) and had a few peculiarities of its own. The planetary transmission involved the use of separate pedals for forward and reverse instead of a gear lever; coupled with a throttle which doubled as a brake (press to go, lift off to stop) and an advance/retard lever mounted on the steering wheel, the Model T was never an easy car to drive, and some states issued separate driving licenses for Fords.

Henry Ford had made himself a reputation on the racetrack with his handbuilt cars *Arrow* and *999*; race success with these was largely how he raised the backing to launch the Ford Motor Company. And the huge quantities of his Model T which began to appear after 1908 meant that it would inevitably be widely used in racing. The early buckboard Ts were everywhere, racing on dirt ovals, the quarter-mile board tracks at county fairs, Pike's Peak, anywhere there was racing.

To begin with, the technique was simply to remove all the bodywork except the hood and a little cowl for the driver to hide behind, sitting in a bucket seat bolted between the chassis rails with the steering column dropped down to suit. Later things became far more sophisticated as extras like grille shells became available, although not from Ford. One of the spinoffs of his success was to give the infant accessory market a huge shot in the arm, and many small companies grew into international corporations supplying the luxuries missing from the very basic Model T. Frontenac started a new ball rolling with their 16-valve conversion for the 178-inch Ford engine.

Later still came the speedster bodies, specially designed and built to replace the bare bones of the buckboard racers and having a graceful, full-fendered elegance of their own. More often than not, these were never intended for racing use but were beautifully made and painted, carefully and luxuriously upholstered inside and fitted with all the luxuries available. Low-slung, with brass radiator and huge brass lamps so characteristic of the Model T, small aero screens to protect the driver and absolutely no other weather protection at all, the Model T Speedsters were as attractively styled as any of the contemporary race cars and marques against which they were matched – despite being the result of mass production rather than careful handcrafting.

During the 19 years it was in production the Model T, in all its variations from two-seater upwards, ran to more than 15 million units – and, although it's incredible that there aren't therefore a great deal more of all kinds left in existence, the Speedsters were comparatively rare, even in the twenties. Because they were built by different companies, even different individuals, their exact number will never be known, except to say that it was all too few. For now, the Speedster is a museum piece, a monument to the genius of one man and to the individuality of mass production.

Ford GT 40

Henry Ford died in 1947, but his first love – of motor racing – continued under Ford Motor Company's banner; in the fifties and sixties, when the US auto industry had its 'gentlemen's agreement' not to go racing, the gentlemen at Ford kept right on keeping on. In fact they were so keen on keeping on that they involved an ex-racing driver with their Total Performance Program.

Forced by a heart condition to retire from racing, Carroll Shelby turned to the manufacture of race cars. He had raced on circuits across the United States and Europe, driven for Porsche, won the 1959 Le Mans 24 Hours for Aston Martin and was more than qualified. His was the idea to combine nimble European chassis and suspension with an American V8. The body and chassis unit was from the AC company at Thames Ditton, England, and the body was an open two-seater with a very long hood and a tiny cramped cockpit perched in front of a short, bobbed deck.

Shelby's choice of engine went to Ford; his proposition arrived at a time when the company was looking to

Made in small numbers, the Le Mans-winning GT40 (*below*) is now so highly prized as a collectors' item that its price has made the construction of fiberglass replicas like the faithfully-detailed KVA (*right*) financially viable.

produce a sportscar anyway – they were already at work on the Mustang. In 1965 the result of this almost unholy alliance had lent a blistering new meaning to the word 'snakebite,' established an automotive benchmark for all time and brought the United States the ultimate motorsport accolade and Ford their first World Manufacturers' Championship. To win the FIA GT Championship Shelby's Cobras had shown their tails to Ferrari at Daytona, Sebring, Oulton Park, Nurburgring, Rossfeld, Rheims and, rubbing salt in the wound, Monza. The only real disappointment had come at Le Mans when the Cobras ran in second behind the red Ferraris, but even in that defeat were the seeds of a future victory; running alongside the Cobras in the 1965 racing season were their stablemates, the first examples of the infant Ford GT.

This project was also partly British, involving the expertise of a number of people like John Wyer and chassis designer Len Bailey, and had been revealed in 1963 when the GT was shown in New York. It went to Le Mans the following year, and again in 1965, and although it set lap records both times none of the cars finished the grueling race.

Although the Cobra had been powered by Ford, it was Shelby who'd won the GT Championship; Ford were anxious to secure their own trophies, and it was this 'mobile testbed,' as they'd called their GT in 1964, which they were relying on. Shelby withdrew the Cobras from competition in 1965 – partly because he could see a certain wisdom in not embarrassing Ford by running rings round them – and from then on they were succeeded on the track by the Ford GT. At first there was little or no joy to be had until, in virtual desperation, the project was passed over to Shelby; in 1966, 1-2-3 wins at Daytona and Sebring were followed in short order by the achievement for which Ford had been looking and for which the GT had been conceived and built. The GT 40, as it was now known since it was 40 inches tall, showed *Il Commendatore* the way home at the 1966 Le Mans with yet another 1-2-3 procession of GT 40s across the line, a fine win which gave Ford their second World Constructors' Championship, this time in both Prototype and Sportscar categories.

There can be no doubt that this is what the cars were built for; mid-engine layout, 427ci V8 and long aerodynamic lines designed for sustained high-speed cruising were blended with the Shelby experience and genius to produce an unstoppable combination.

Only a very few – 31 – of the GT 40s were built as road cars (*below*). Most of the surviving race cars are museum pieces, although some appear in special classic events. The replicas (KVA, *right*) make road use a practical possibility.

Homologation rules meant that very few cars needed to be built; in the whole lifespan of the GT 40 only 100 were made and only 31 of these were roadgoing versions, 'detuned' to a maximum 165mph out of the stock 335hp 427.

In 1967 Ford returned to Le Mans and the Gurney/Foyt GT 40 demonstrated the difference between a road car and race car; it averaged a constant 135.48mph for 24 consecutive hours. Allowing for pitstops and for the fact that the Sarthe circuit does not permit full-throttle driving all the way round (far from it, in fact), the GT must have hit its 250mph-plus maximum speed often, and quickly.

In fact it was so impressive that the FIA changed the rules for the next year, limiting prototypes to a three-liter capacity and allowing so-called production sports-cars (minimum manufacturing run of 50) a maximum five-liter capacity.

Shelby had already worked his magic on the Ford 289ci V8, which fitted comfortably under the capacity limit. In 1968 Ford won the 1000kms at Spa and Monza, the BOAC 500 at Brands Hatch, the Endurance race at Watkins Glen, the Le Mans 24 Hours and the World Sportscar Manufacturers' Championship. A year later, in 1969, Jackie Ickx and Jackie Oliver won Ford's fourth Le Mans title.

By 1970 Carroll Shelby had asked Ford to release him from Total Performance; the Cobra was dead, the Shelby Mustangs were in their final year and 'Performance' was a dirty word in Detroit and Washington. The GT 40 race program was axed at the same time, and those cars which survive today are mostly museum pieces, although a tiny number reappear at historic race events – generally for the pleasure of a quiet spin round the circuit rather than a competitive race – and there are still a few road cars in existence.

They are genuine, appreciating and expensive collectors' items, worth more than the most expensive new Rolls-Royce – say around $100,000 – and worth every penny. The seats are virtually horizontal, the power surge incredible, and the smooth boost through the gears (58mph in first, 90 in second, 127 in third, 142 in fourth and up to 165 and beyond in fifth) gives the GT 40, as John Wyer described it when the cars were first built in Slough, England, all those years ago, 'more than average performance.'

Hispano-Suiza

Although their origins were Spanish, the Hispano-Suizas became best known as French vehicles, being built simultaneously in both Barcelona and the French factory at Bois-Colombes, near Paris.

The original company, La Fabrica Automoviles la Hispano-Suiza, was formed in Barcelona in 1904. The Spanish derivation is obvious, the Swiss element resulting from the nationality of designer Mark Birkigt. He was a railway engineer who turned – like Royce and Bentley – to the motorcar. Like them, he also was responsible for a number of automotive firsts, including hollow, water-cooled brake shoes (1906), a supercharger (1912) and even a shaft-drive arrangement which used the vehicle's rear springs to take up the torque thus created.

The racing Hispano-Suizas made their mark for the first time in the 1910 Coupe des Voiturettes, using a four-cylinder engine in a lightweight chassis. King Alfonso XIII of Spain was so impressed by the victory that he ordered a car for himself, and the factory obliged him with a new car designated the T15 and named the Alfonso XIII in his honor. Similar to the Mercer Raceabout, it remained in production until 1920 when it was succeeded by a newer and much larger car. During World War I Hispano-Suiza had made aero engines in vast numbers. Powering the Nieuports and the Spads of the French *escadrilles*, 50,000 of the big engines had served half the aces on the Western Front, including René Fonck, Georges Guynemer and Eddie Rickenbacker. After the war the squadron emblem which had been painted on Georges Guynemer's Spad, the stork, was adopted as the radiator mascot for the Hispano-Suiza cars.

The airplane engine had been a large V8, but the first car powerplant built after the war was a straight six of 6.5 liters capacity. However its heritage was clearly apparent, and it used the same shaft-drive format for the overhead camshaft, which operated directly on to the top of the valve stems. In fact this engine was half of a projected V12 aero engine, which possibly accounts

for its immense strength. The seven-bearing crankshaft was machined out of a solid 700lb forged steel billet; when finished, the whole weighed in at a mere 95 pounds.

The cylinders were likewise of forged steel, threaded on the outside and then screwed into an aluminum cooling jacket. The compression ratio was low – 4.5:1 – but the engine delivered 135hp at 2400 rpm. Later enlarged to nearer eight liters (in the 'Boulogne' model), the engine was producing a fairly substantial output which could lift the same lightweight chassis another 10mph to take it over the 100mph barrier.

It was not only the engine which featured clever engineering and one or two innovations. There were two batteries fitted as standard, and they could be selected individually or used together for really efficient cold starting. The fuze panel was mounted behind a small glass window, and each fuze had its own telltale lamp which remained lit all the time there was current running through.

And at a time when vehicle braking systems were far from sophisticated – rod-operated rear-wheel brakes were the most common variety – the Hispano-Suiza was fitted with powerful four-wheel brakes with iron liners inside finned alloy drums. Even more unusual, they were power-assisted by a servo driven from the side of the gearbox. It was a clever arrangement which would later appear on a number of other cars, notably those built by Rolls-Royce.

The gearbox was a manual device with one extremely low ratio, an intermediate which the manufacturer recommended for pulling away from a standstill, and direct drive. The handbook suggested that this should be engaged as soon as the car was rolling and then that the gearbox should be left entirely alone except in emergencies.

The car it was originally fitted to, the Hispano-Suiza H6, became the star of the 1919 Paris Motor Show. It was built, as was the custom of the period, as a rolling chassis/engine, and bodywork was left to the individual

customer. It was originally intended that it should carry light touring or town-car coachwork, but the smooth power and superb stopping ability of the servo brakes made it an ideal basis for what were then just being termed sportscars. Liquor millionaire André Dubonnet entered his H6 for the Georges Boillot Cup in 1921 and his win led to the emergence the following year of a team of Hispano-Suiza cars being entered, this time using what would become the Boulogne model with larger 7982cc engines and a shorter wheelbase. They won in 1922 and 1923, and from 1924 the engine was made generally available in touring cars.

Dubonnet also entered the 1924 Targa Florio in his Hispano, an event for which it was eminently unsuited. But the reliability of the big eight-liter powerplant brought him home in a worthy seventh place. And much later Woolf 'Babe' Barnato, famous as one of the 'Bentley Boys,' covered 300 miles round Brooklands at an average of 92mph in a similar Hispano-Suiza.

In 1931 Hispano-Suiza bought out the Ballot company and began the manufacture of expensive, up-market luxury cars. The V12 engine finally appeared, although by now the overhead cam had given way to more usual pushrods. With a perfectly square bore/stroke relationship – 100mm × 100mm – the first V12 had a capacity of 9427cc, but later versions with a longer, 120mm stroke, were up to a massive 11,300cc – almost 1000cc per cylinder. Weighing in at around three tons, these brutish vehicles were capable of a 110mph top speed and acceleration from 0-60mph in 12 seconds – all without exceeding 3000rpm!

Quiet and luxurious they may have been, but they were also expensive. During the thirties they were priced at more than $40,000, second only to the extravagant Bugatti Royale.

The French factory closed down in 1939, but the Barcelona works carried on until 1943. After becoming part of the Enasa bus company, the same factory turned out a small run of the interesting but short-lived Pegaso sportscar in the fifties but the magic had long gone.

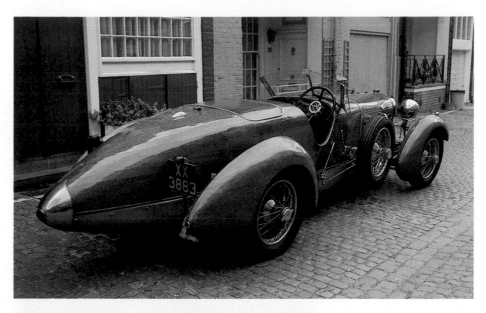

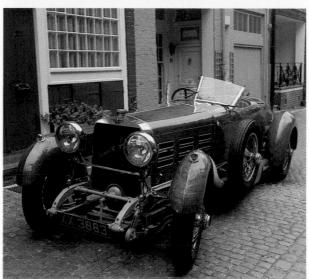

All pictures: A Hispano-Suiza Torpedo convertible of 1925, typical of the sporty types the company developed in the twenties.

Above: Bodied by British coachbuilders Gurney and Nutting, this 8-liter Hispano-Suiza Boulogne dates from 1928 as the company turned away from racing activities to build luxury cars.

ISO

The idea of putting a large American V8 engine into a European-designed sportscar has been around for a while. Jean Daninos began the trend with his Facel Vega, but it was soon seized upon by others. Among them were soon to be numbered several members of the Detroit fraternity, who could see at once the potential of combining the allure of the fleet-footed European cars with a powerful, recognized, relatively commonplace and therefore easily serviceable domestic V8.

Shelby's Cobra was probably the most successful combination, but there were others, like the Ford/De Tomaso setup, who tried. And there were still others who went solo, like Jensen and Bristol in Britain.

To a large extent these international marriages of convenience were frequently less than blissful. Beyond any doubt the cars which emerged from the unions were possessed of a certain amount of mystique as a result of their occasionally dubious parentage, but the nature of the offspring was frequently suspect.

In part this can be ascribed to the fact that the bulk of the partnerships thus formed were between America and Italy – and while the Italians were more than capable of blessing the fruits of the union with all the excitable, vibrant and sensuous nature which the Latin half of their lineage might be expected to dictate, the American half could not put in the sophisticated reliability of the mass-production line after the cars were built. In short, there was frequently a build quality and reliability problem, and it was generally the American dealerships who were left to pick up the bits.

There may also have been other problems. Consider the activities of one Giotti Bizzarrini during the early part of the sixties. Having established a reputation as a skillful engineer with Ferrari and Alfa Romeo, he was simultaneously working on designs for Lamborghini (the 350GT), for Iso (the Rivolta and Grifo) and his own race car, the Bizzarrini GT Strada 5300.

His own car, front engine and rear-wheel drive, was on a platform chassis with bodywork by Bertone and ran a GM V8 powerplant. Much of the design and many of the components appeared in the other cars he was working on at the same time, and at one stage it appeared that the body shape would actually be used by Iso for their Grifo. In any case the Strada and the Grifo turned out to be very similar cars.

During the fifties the Iso company had been turning out large numbers of cars which have since become – on a small scale – collectors' cars in their own right. But the Iso Isetta bubble car could hardly have been more different to the Iso Rivolta which appeared at the 1962 Turin Motor Show.

Powered by a 327ci V8, with four or five-speed ZF manual or GM automatic gearbox, the Rivolta was a conventional front-engine, rear-drive four-seat GT with alloy coachwork by Bertone. The Detroit engine gave it a highly-respectable top speed of 140mph, which put it very firmly alongside the best which was coming from the Italian exoticar makers of the time, but the Rivolta lacked the history and the glamor to compete on the same level. In one respect, although the use of a familiar engine/driveline layout gave it a reliability the others may have lacked, it seemed that the whizzy V12s of Modena were half the attraction when it came to choosing a sportscar.

Above and below: Designed by Bizzarrini, the Iso Rivolta, elegant and successful enough in its own right, formed a platform for successive Iso designs.

power spread of either 300 or 365hp. Weighing in at around 3000lbs, depending on which engine was fitted, the Grifo was fractionally lighter than the car from which it was developed.

Once again the body was a Bertone design, and this time it was a no-compromise two-door, two-seat fastback with a dominating frontal aspect and a massively long hood. But it lived up to its appearance in no uncertain way, and with the big-block rat motor for power it could pound the standing quarter in just under 15 seconds and carry on to an impressive 160mph, putting it well towards the top of the performance ladder and guaranteeing supercar status.

In later years, the Grifo was fitted with the biggest of the big blocks, and packing a 454 it could stretch out to top speeds in excess of 170mph. At the same time the front-end treatment was sharpened up and given concealed headlamps which brought its appearance more up to date. In the end, though, it was the fuel crisis which killed it off, robbing it of the big-inch, high-compression engines which were necessary to attain such stupendous performance levels.

The Grifo was axed in 1970, giving way to Iso's modern cars, the Ghia-designed Fidia, which replaced the Rivolta as Iso's four-seater, and the Bertone-designed Lele. This 2+2 two-door used the longer Rivolta chassis and although Iso stuck to their GM V8 engines neither car could take the place of the Grifo. In any case the fuel crisis was tightening its grip on the West and especially the auto industry, and eventually Iso became another casualty of international disagreement about oil; the last Iso was built in 1974.

The Rivolta sold well, though, even gaining itself a reprieve; when it was due to be phased out and replaced by the Fidia in 1968 the order book was full enough to keep it in production until 1970.

Before that, though, the Rivolta chassis formed the base of other Iso supercar contenders, and there's no doubt that the highlight was the 1965 production version of the Iso Grifo which had been shown at Turin in 1963. The same platform chassis, although slightly shorter, formed its base, and the same front-engine, rear-drive layout was used. Independent front suspension and De Dion back axle were standard, as were four-wheel disk brakes. Once again there was a choice between ZF manual and GM auto transmission, and the engines varied between the same 327ci Corvette powerplant or the far more impressive 427, giving it a

Isotta Fraschini

Cesare Isotta and Vincenzo Fraschini formed their company in 1900 and, with a degree of logic, called it Isotta-Fraschini. Within a single year their first car, designed by Oreste Fraschini, was on display at the 1901 Milan Exposition. With a single cylinder it developed 5hp, and though that may not sound a great deal it should be remembered that at this period the automobile was in its early infancy. While motorsport was equally undeveloped the Isotta-Fraschini company moved straight ahead into competition.

As a way of adding perspective it must be remembered that Utah was barely five years previously admitted to the Union, and this was the same year that Queen Victoria died and Theodore Roosevelt became President after McKinley was assassinated.

A single-cylinder motor vehicle producing 5hp was therefore no laughing matter, and indeed the Isotta-Fraschinis began at once to establish themselves as

vehicles to be reckoned with. In 1902 Vincenzo Fraschini had driven to second place in the Sassi-Superga hillclimb, and by 1906 the Isotta-Fraschini was an important and well-known make, introducing three new models (one of them a straight six of 90hp) at the Paris Salon that year. By the outbreak of World War I there had been more than 40 models from Isotta, and more race success.

Winners of the 1908 Targa Florio, they had competed in the 1913 Indy 500 as well. They were to Italy what Rolls-Royce were to Britain, Hispano-Suiza were to France. Their cars were, it must be said, usually rather smaller with capacities to match and typically falling into the 'voiturette' class of racing.

But after 1918, as they turned once again to car manufacture, the small, light racers had been replaced by large, luxurious and expensive tourers. After the opening of a New York showroom in 1924 Isotta-

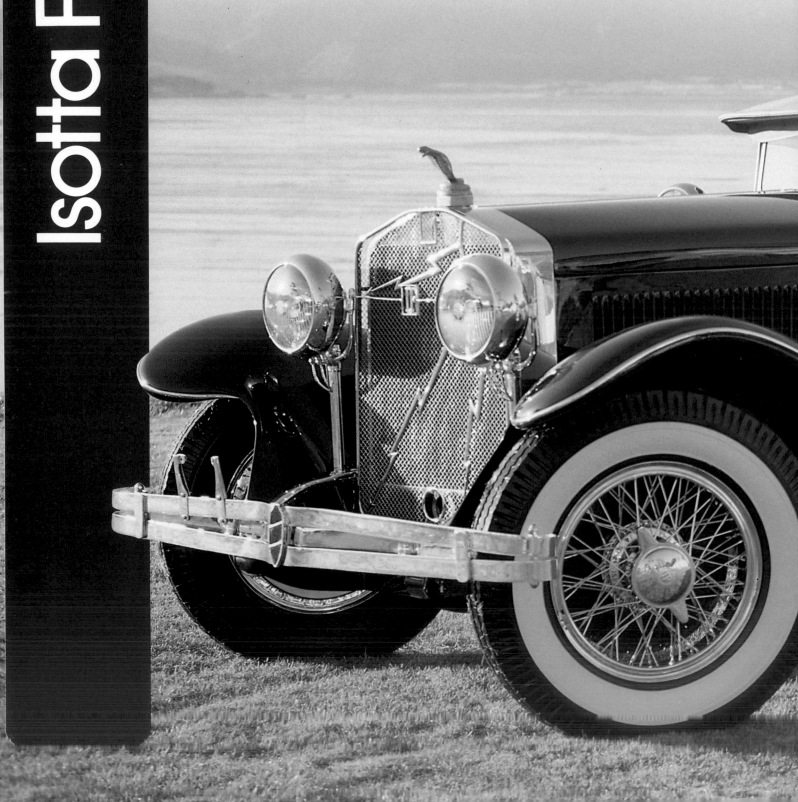

Fraschini became extremely popular among the denizens of the movie industry, then in the process of moving from New York to the sunlit orange groves Cecil B De Mille had discovered north of Los Angeles in a place called Hollywood. Their new customers included Clara Bow, Jack Dempsey, Rudolf Valentino and even redoubtable press magnate W R Hearst.

None of the postwar cars were ever likely to be the equal of the monster IM and KM. The IM was blessed with a four-cylinder engine of an incredible 12 liters (or three liters per cylinder!), but was succeeded by the smaller KM, which had been in production immediately prior to the outbreak of hostilities. Its four-cylinder single ohc engine had four valves per cylinder and developed a healthy 140hp at a mere 1800rpm. In order to accomplish this, each of its cylinders had a swept volume of 2750cc – that's 167 cubic inches – giving it an 11-liter (671ci) total capacity. Four-wheel brakes (two on a pedal, two controlled by an outside lever, plus a pedal-operated transmission brake) were – necessarily – supplied, and the KM weighed in at more than 5000lbs. It was also capable of lapping the Indy circuit in 1 minute 50 seconds, which is no mean achievement.

Postwar vehicles were somewhat more refined, although technical advance was still part and parcel of the Isotta appeal. In 1920 they put the world's first straight-eight engine into production in their Tipo 8. The aluminum engine was a single casting, the near-hemispherical heads were two castings. Nine-bearing crank, aluminum pistons, overhead valves and six liters gave 80hp at 2200rpm. Four-wheel brakes were aided by a mechanical servo, and the chassis was a substantial 145 inches. It stayed in production for five years until replaced in 1925 by the Tipo 8A.

This basically offered buyers a much wider choice, which began with the option of the 'sports' chassis, which was shorter at only 134 inches. The brake servo was now vacuum-operated (the system still in use today) and there were three engine alternatives now available. Now enlarged to more than seven liters, the stock engine had two carburetors and gave up to 120hp. After that came the modified Spinto engine and finally the Super Spinto which, thanks to improved breathing from modified manifolding and valves, was good for

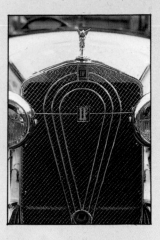

Above: The distinctive Isotta radiator and emblem.

Below: The superb Tipo 8ASS from 1933.

150hp and a claimed top speed of over 100mph in the short-chassis version.

In keeping with the industry of the time – certainly at this level of price and performance – the Isotta-Fraschini was bodied by a coachbuilder away from the factory. Left to their own devices, Isotta sent their cars to the famous *carrozeria* of Italy – Castagna in particular – but through the New York office a number of them went to Le Baron and others. This kind of treatment made them extremely expensive cars to own and an

Left: By the time Isotta-Fraschini had followed the traditional pattern of graduating to upmarket formal limousines their price had climbed as well, and the Castagna-bodied cars commanded prices equal to the likes of Rolls-Royce, Hispano-Suiza and Bugatti.

Italian-bodied 8A could cost $15,000 – about the same as a Springfield Rolls-Royce – at a time when Henry Ford was selling his Model T by the hundred thousand for only a few hundred dollars and America was rushing headlong into the Depression.

Coinciding with the worst years came the Tipo 8B, which was little more than a slightly modified 8A with a heavier chassis, coil ignition – dispensing with the magneto – and a semi-automatic gearbox instead of the three-speed manual which had been fitted as a unit with the engine on the Tipo 8 and 8A.

It was really something of a swansong for Isotta-Fraschini. Swallowed up in World War II, they emerged with the Tipo 8C in 1947. Packing a 3.5-liter rear-mounted V8, it created something of a stir at the Paris Salon that year but never went into production, and Isotta-Fraschini became another name added to the casualty lists.

Jaguar

At 21 years of age William Lyons, destined to become the honored Sir William, elder statesman of the British car industry and known to close associates simply as 'Bill,' joined forces with William Walmsley, who had been building motorcycle sidecars with some success in Stockport, Cheshire. They formed the Swallow Sidecar Company in Blackpool in 1922, producing sidecars of great refinement and elegance. The economy end of the infant car-manufacturing business prospered at that time, and as people like Herbert Austin began to build extremely basic and cheap motor cars to replace the demand for motorcycles, so Swallow moved into coachbuilding. By 1926 this side of their affairs had prospered to the extent that the company was renamed the Swallow Sidecar and Coachbuilding Company, the change being swiftly followed by a move to larger premises in Coventry.

With the move came the first car they could truly call their own. Based on a Standard chassis and engine, the SS1 was a low, swoopy sedan of immense grace and exceedingly small price – £300. It was followed by the even cheaper SS2, which cost a mere £200. Greater success followed, and in 1934 the company changed its name again, this time for the last-but-one time, becoming SS Cars Limited.

It was shortly after the change that SS gained the experience and genius of Harry Weslake, who designed an ohv conversion for the Standard engine they were still using and gave it a vast power increase. Because of its claimed 90mph top speed the car was designated SS90, and was a sportscar of considerable ability and appeal. It was completely overshadowed by the model which followed it, however, the classic SS100 being easily capable of a 100mph top speed.

Left: The SS100 is commonly regarded as being the best product of the prewar Jaguar factory, embodying all the features of the period and set a style which is still identified with classic sportscar design. A 1937 example is pictured.

Above left and above: The 1938-model SS100.

Below: The XK120 was the car on which the postwar Jaguar success was founded, even though its production was almost an oversight and it was an addition to a range of already-designed family sedans.

Left: By 1952 the rear fender skirts had gone, giving the XK120 a truly graceful appearance.

Right: This is probably the most desirable and attractive of the entire XK series, the XK150 coupé from 1959.

Below: The famous Jaguar badge proudly confirms the company's connection with the city of Coventry.

Bottom: The shortlived XK140 of 1954, seen here in hardtop form.

By now William Lyons was designing for the company, and his touch with car design was every bit as delicate and elegant as Walmsley's had been with those original sidecars. The SS100 was the absolute pinnacle of the prewar SS cars, with a full-fendered sweep to its lines which set off the squarish front perfectly, lending elegance to brute strength to make the ideal combination for a sportscar. The mechanics of the vehicle were hardly at the forefront of contemporary technology, however, and independent suspension was yet to be a feature of SS design. Powerplant was still an old Standard pushrod engine with headwork by Weslake; low weight and good breathing gave the performance, while handling was definitely of the very basic tail-out and tire-squeal variety.

But it was from this heritage that the legendary postwar XK series cars were born as the company changed names for the last time. Designed for Jaguar Cars by Claude Baily, Bill Heynes and Walter Hassan – reputedly on the back of a cigarette packet as the engineers sat on a factory roof and watched Birmingham being bombed flat during the war – the new engine was destined to become the stock Jaguar powerplant for the next 30 years, thanks to its efficient, smooth and powerful character. Once again it benefited from the skills of Harry Weslake, who provided a light-alloy

Above: Probably the best-known of all the Jaguars, the D-type was the clear forerunner of the XKE. Genuine examples, like this 1954 model, command prices well above $100,000.

cylinder head with dual cams and angled valves in a hemispherical combustion chamber. Two SU carburetors fed the 3.5-liter straight six, and it produced 160hp in stock form.

It was William Lyons who felt that this engine deserved a worthier home than good sedan cars, and that in any case the old traditions demanded a sportscar; most of the design work was his, and the result created a sensation when it first appeared in 1948. The low-slung body was mounted on a fairly standard box-frame chassis, independent front suspension was by torsion bars and the solid rear axle was carried on leaf springs. It had huge 12-inch diameter drum brakes and needed them; in what Jaguar claimed was stock trim (although there was more than one skeptic) but minus windshield and soft top, an XK120 was timed at 132mph over the flying mile.

The soft-top was followed by a closed coupé in 1951, and there was to follow a series of Le Mans wins which established Jaguar as one of the greatest names in motor sport for the period. This giant reputation, allied to a $4000 sticker price, ensured vast export sales for Jaguar, and 90 percent of factory output was exported, mostly to America, where its challenge was eventually taken up by the Corvette. In 1954 the XK120 was replaced by the shortlived XK140, but by this time the circuit racers were already laying down the formula for the future.

The racing C-type and D-type Jaguars made their own legends in the hands of people like Stirling Moss, and the string of successes Jaguar enjoyed totally established the supremacy of disk brakes over drum brakes if they achieved nothing else. Introduced on the C-type in 1952, they made the roadgoing range with the 1957 XK150, probably the best-looking Jaguar ever made. Unitary construction, doing away with the hefty chassis, had been a feature of the 2.4-liter Jaguar sedans from 1955 onwards, and most of these lessons were applied to the XKE on its introduction in 1961.

This retained the 3.8-liter powerplant from the XK150, introduced electric cooling fans, borrowed the IRS setup which had first seen action on the Briggs Cunningham experimental Le Mans car of 1960, and featured the sleekest body shape yet seen anywhere in the world. It also delivered numbing performance; 150mph top speed, 0-100mph in less than 16 seconds and 0-125mph in less than 30 seconds. Available as a roadster or a two-seat coupé, the XKE cost a mere $2800 at a time when no Ferrari could be bought for less than $8000 (although exchange rates have changed considerably since then, and it is probably fairer to say that the XKE then was $4800 and the Ferrari $14,000).

In 1964 the XKE grew a 4.2-liter engine and then in 1971 it was fitted with the 5.3 liter V12 which is now the stock Jaguar powerplant for their current sports tourer, the XJS, and the endurance racers which are creeping back onto race circuits under the guiding hand of Tom Walkinshaw. The XKE was finally phased out in 1975, and though the race cars are in high demand – try buying a D-type for less than $100,000 – the XKE is perhaps even more highly prized than the 120, 140 or 150 models.

Above: The XK150 in convertible bodystyle is a goodlooking car in its own right.

Top right: A 1955 D-type with tailfin added as the effects of aerodynamics on high-speed ability and handling began to be appreciated.

Right: Front-on, the D-type's swoopy lines are clearly ahead of the bulk of its slabbier contemporaries.

Below: Also from 1955, this D-type 'short-nose' features a slightly different front-end treatment. The influence of these cars is still visible on Jaguar experimentals and race cars years later – like the XJ13, for example.

John Dodd 'Rolls-Royce'

When the Supermarine company needed an engine to power their Schneider Trophy-chasing seaplanes they ended up dealing with Henry Royce. He based his work on the American Liberty engines of 1918 and produced a V12 powerplant after £100,000 from Lady Houston had funded Supermarine's bid to secure the Trophy in perpetuity. The S6B was designed by Reginald Mitchell and used a Rolls-Royce engine which was later developed into the world-famous and world-beating Merlin. This powered the Hawker Hurricane, de Havilland Mosquito, Avro Lancaster, North American Mustang, a selection of tanks and, of course, the elegant – and Mitchell-designed – Spitfire.

The Supermarine S6 used a Rolls-Royce V12 engine which developed almost 2000hp; its slightly larger successor, the S6B, used a similar engine, now developed to give 2350hp, and it was this which won the Schneider Trophy for Britain in 1931. Much of the power developed for this engine was a result of chemical fuels which were suitable for racing but hardly practical for everyday use.

Consequently when the 27-liter V12 Merlin engine went into service with the Royal Air Force it was in somewhat detuned form, running on straight aviation spirit. Technical advances in the United States resulted in the standardization of 100-octane gasoline, in which form it went to a much lower rev limit, produced a rather more conservative 1000hp and was likely to last a great deal longer between major rebuilds. In this form it gave the Supermarine Spitfire, with which the RAF entered the Battle of Britain, a maximum speed of 362mph, although later versions were faster.

After the war ended, as the jet gained its ultimate superiority over the piston engine, the vast numbers of Spitfires – and other Merlin-engined aircraft – slowly disappeared, until the few flying examples which remain command staggeringly high prices; a Spitfire at auction in 1984 was withdrawn at £300,000 because it had failed to make its reserve of £350,000.

In the early seventies, John Dodd set himself the task of matching a Merlin engine to a transmission which could transform its massive torque into roadgoing tractability. The first signs that he may have succeeded came when strange stories began to creep into the press. They concerned baffled and curious motorists who had lost the doors of their Ferrari/Porsche/other supercar to a large and ponderous-looking device which had passed them on the freeway/*autobahn*/*autostrada* at a speed generally reckoned as being somewhere in excess of 200mph.

There were even rumours that the German Police had asked Rolls-Royce to refrain from testing their new car on the *autobahns*. Even though they're limit-free, speeds over 200mph were reckoned to be vaguely anti-social. Rolls-Royce denied involvement. This amusing tale may or may not be true, but it was certainly true that John Dodd had fixed wheels to a Merlin engine and – since it was Rolls-Royce built – had also fixed a Rolls-Royce radiator shell, complete with Spirit of Ecstasy, to the front of a massive two-door sedan body created for him by Fibreglass Repairs of Bromley.

The press eventually tracked John Dodd down, and much was made of his monstrous vehicle – which resembled Lady Penelope's pink convertible used in the *Thunderbirds* TV series – although he admitted having problems with the flywheel coming unstuck at speeds 'approaching 200 mph.'

Then disaster struck, and the car was almost completely destroyed by fire. But the chassis and engine remained, and Dodd set to work again. This time

Right: The interior of *The Beast* features less dials than a Spitfire, showing that the big V12 doesn't need constant nursing.

Below: The body is the vehicle's second, after the original was destroyed by fire.

Fibreglass Repairs built a two-door station-wagon body, still with the Rolls-Royce radiator shell at the end of its massive hood. Dodd had successfully mastered all the transmission problems, and hooked the huge engine up to a GM Turbo 400 which he had strengthened and modified to take the output.

The big V12 in the new car, called *The Beast* by Dodd, is of uncertain vintage and history, although it's likely that it has never powered anything more glamorous than a tank. Top output is 'only' about 750hp, but that's developed at 2500rpm – the tachometer is redlined at 2800 – and the car will make 140mph at 1250rpm in top, which gives a fair indication of its theoretical top speed. In contrast, tickover for the superbly-balanced V12 is 120rpm.

And although *The Beast* is licenced for street use, not everybody is happy that it should be used on the street. Aside from going over the UK legal limit of 70mph at about 6-700rpm and various exoticar owners being extremely upset when they were blown away by something the size of a Mack truck, Rolls-Royce themselves were decidedly unhappy about Dodd's use of their radiator grille and emblem.

Their displeasure was vented in a court case in 1983, during which John Dodd displayed *The Beast*'s supreme unreliability by regularly breaking down on his way to court each day, confirming once and for all that the Merlin engine was simply never designed for the hustle of city traffic. But the panache and bravado required to flaunt your misdeeds beneath the very nose of authority attracted Dodd precisely the kind of publicity he was hoping for, and the case was faithfully reported in the national press.

It was a legal tussle in the great traditions of that fast-disappearing species, the Great British Eccentric. Judgement went against Dodd, however, and he and the car promptly disappeared from sight. Current rumors place Dodd in extradition-free Spain, although they do not locate *The Beast*, which is a great pity. With or without the radiator shell and emblem, there's something about a 27-liter V12 which commands respect...

Left: The Beast's vaguely familiar-looking front end, with that contentious Rolls-Royce grille and emblem.

Above: Back-end treatment is clean and simple. It's only the vast length of the rest of the car (*right*) which makes it look somewhat unwieldy.

Lagonda

The history of the auto industry is full of people who emigrated to the United States and then made excellent motor cars and also their fortunes; Buick was Scottish, the Duesenberg brothers German, Henry Ford's parents Irish, the two Chevrolets Swiss-born French residents who emigrated to Canada before moving to New York. Wilbur Gunn took the reverse route; born in Springfield, Ohio, he moved to England where he built his first single-cylinder motorcycle on the front lawn of his house near Staines.

As he got better and better at building them he naturally progressed, and in 1904 the first of his 'tricars' appeared. Gunn named it after his home town of Lagonda Creek (Lagonda is Indian, and means 'smooth-running stream'). From there he moved on to four-wheel cars, the first of which was finished in 1906. Always sturdy – Lagondas won a number of long-distance and reliability trials, starting with the London-Edinburgh Gold Medal in 1908 – the cars were also progressive; the 1909 Lagonda was the first British car to combine an all-steel body and chassis.

In 1910 Lagonda performed well in the Moscow-St Petersburg Trial and sold well among Russian nobility,

including Tsar Nicholas II. During World War I the factory in Staines turned to the maufacture of munitions, and many Foden steam-wagons bore the Lagonda name. But Gunn realised that after the war the demand would be for small and inexpensive cars; his design for such a vehicle had in fact been ready in 1913. Easily manufactured, it was of monocoque construction with a high-performance 11hp ohv engine; in production once the war was ended, it competed successfully in trials. The engine output was increased as the twenties arrived and it evolved into the 11.9 and then the 12/24. In 1921 it won the Light Car Trophy, covering a distance of 79.19 miles in an hour.

By 1925 the desire to build a bigger, more powerful car had resurfaced, and Arthur Davidson designed a four-cylinder two-liter of some 14hp, with two chain-driven 'underhead' camshafts. This peculiar arrangement included an enormously long intake manifold and the breathing was so poor that the car only performed properly with the addition of a Cozette supercharger.

Left: The 1932 2-liter Lagonda; with its low chassis, this was the 'speed' model.

Below left: The Lagonda's tidily laid-out engine compartment with single SU carburetor and (*below*) an almost modern-looking interior, with parking brake and shift lever at right.

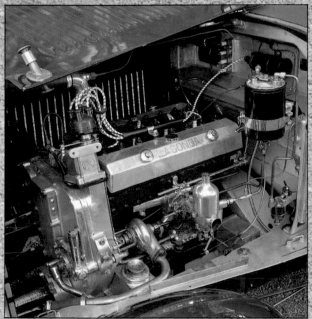

Above: The truly imposing 3-liter Lagonda from 1930. The dash (*left*) contains complete instrumentation and a full set of informative plaques. The ignition advance/retard is mounted on the steering wheel hub.

In blown form, with the low chassis and light fabric touring body with cycle fenders, the 1927 Speed Model became an extremely popular car. Bentley success at Le Mans had prompted a demand for high-speed tourers capable of competing in the kind of road-racing events which then dominated the motor-racing calendar, and the Lagondas were a way of achieving this without going to the expense of a Bentley. The supercharged two-liter was capable of 90mph and 20mpg, so it had the speed to compete with bigger cars.

By 1930 there was a three-liter six as well as the four-pot Speed Model, and then a two-liter six which had a Crossley engine with a normal ohv arrangement instead of the peculiar dual-camshaft layout of the Lagonda engine.

In 1931 Rolls-Royce bought the Bentley company from Woolf 'Babe' Barnato who, together with the input of the amateur 'Bentley Boys,' had kept the company going through the heady years of success at Le Mans. When 'W O' met Henry Royce after the takeover the meeting was less than amicable; Bentley reminded Royce that when he had been an engineering apprentice with the Great Northern Railway at Doncaster, Royce had been little more than a 'gopher' in the Peterborough engine sheds. There seemed to be little requirement for Bentley's services after that, and he parted from the company which bore his name.

Meanwhile Alan Good had stepped between Rolls-Royce and their next intended purchase, and it was he who called in W O to help with the big six cylinder

Left, right and below: The 1935 Lagonda M45, a 4.5-liter touring car.

Below right and bottom: The 1937 LG45 utilized the same chassis as the M45; a drophead coupé is illustrated.

4.5-liter Lagondas in 1935. These Meadows-engined cars had come second and third in the RAC Tourist Trophy unlimited class the previous year and in 1935 won at Le Mans, covering 1868.42 miles in the 24 Hours at an average speed of 77.85mph. Bentley first altered the springing on the big cars to help their handling and then improved engine aspiration, allowing them to rev more freely up to 4000rpm. As time went by he also added hydraulic brakes to replace the mechanical items, and later still modified the suspension again so that the 1938 cars boasted independent front suspension.

By this time W O was moving on to produce for Lagonda the 4.5-liter V12 which would power the 1938-39 race cars, developing 180hp and capable of lapping Brooklands at 128mph. It was the V12 which was the first closed production car to exceed 100mph, and in 1938 one sedan covered 101.5 miles in an hour, including a stop to change a tire. Although two stock production-line V12 Lagondas finished third and fourth in the 1939 Le Mans 24 Hours, the outbreak of war meant that only a very few ever saw production and the big Lagondas of the thirties were represented on the roads by the 4.5-liter LG45s.

Bodywork on these varied somewhat, from the two-seat boat-tails with cycle fenders that made their dominant presence felt on racetracks all over Europe to the elegant full-fendered tourers. All shared the same imposing radiator, flanked by massive driving lamps, while the strapped hood concealed the long 4453cc straight six with side-draft carburetor which could propel the car up to around 100mph.

In Britain between the wars there were few cars which could properly be described as luxury high-performance tourers. After 1931 Rolls-Royce led the way with their 4.5-liter Bentleys built at Derby, while the 4.3 Alvis tourer was perhaps slightly faster than the Lagonda. But those three were the glamorous names in the British motor industry, and at a time when flag-waving and national pride were far more commonplace and acceptable than perhaps they are now there was no doubt that Wilbur Gunn's Lagonda earned the right to be a genuine flag-bearer. Perhaps the truth of this is reflected in the collectability of the prewar Lagondas; in mid 1984 an LG45 Rapide in need of a complete rebuild was sold at auction for $25,000.

All pictures The excellent V12 engine designed by W O Bentley found its best home in these drophead coupés.

At the end of World War II Ferruccio Lamborghini satisfied his desire for fast cars by tuning the cars produced by Fiat. He ran a small machine-shop at the time but gradually turned to the manufacture of tractors as his major occupation, thus starting a vast industrial empire which, by the sixties, was in a secure enough financial position for Lamborghini to turn his attention to other sidelines. He began by building himself a car, mostly because he thought he could do it better than Maserati or Ferrari.

The chassis was multi-tubular, the front-mounted engine a 3.5-liter V12 with four overhead camshafts and six Weber carburetors; driving through the ubiquitous ZF five-speed into a limited-slip rearend it produced 360hp, and the coil-and-wishbone independent suspension meant that all the power was usable.

The bodywork was a closed coupé designed by Gian Paolo Dallara and featuring retractable headlamps at the leading edge of the now-typical flat curve of the Italian sportscar; this was 1963, 20 years before anything built in the United States – other than the Corvette – featured similarly clean aerodynamic lines.

But the first Lamborghini was a one-off for the man who built tractors, and although he went on to build around 200 of them over the next two years it was by no means accepted as a supercar by those who traditionally built them around Modena. It was in 1965, at the Turin Motor Show, that Lamborghini crossed the dividing line between the rich man's toy and the specialist sportscar maker. Originally a Dallara-designed spyder, the Miura T400 which went into production for the 1966 model year was a mid-engined coupé with a slightly bigger, four-liter version of the ohc V12 slung transversely behind the two seats, driving the rear wheels by spur gears. This time Lamborghini built his own gearboxes and rear axles, the frame was a box-section affair beneath the monocoque body and the whole lot weighed in at 2700lbs. The V12 now gave 385hp, which was enough to boost the small coupé up to a tremendous 180mph and made it one of the fastest road cars ever – certainly enough to place it right alongside the best that wore the prancing horse of the neighboring Ferrari factory.

The Miura was instantly accepted into the supercar league and remains one of the best-looking vehicles Lamborghini ever gave his name to; certainly it was the most uncompromising and might easily have been designed for endurance racing at Le Mans rather than road use. Critics of the marque will say that this is reflected in the high levels of cockpit noise created as all that machinery whirred into vibrant life inches behind the driver's ears, something which is typical of high-performance mid-engine sportscars. Fans of thoroughbred Italian machinery, however, will say they'd rather listen to that than the hifi – or, indeed, the conversation of their passengers.

Although the Miura stayed in production for nine years, during which time they were built at the rate of two a week, Lamborghini brought its follow-up into production within two years, and this time he went back to the front-engine layout of his first GT, although concessions to those who liked their motoring accompanied by civilized noise levels ended there; the Espada retained the four-liter V12, complete with whizzy overhead cams and multiple-choke carburetors greedily sucking air.

The 2+2 version of the Espada was the Jarama, with a longer roofline and more glass area for back seat passengers, and with the Miura in full production the factory could afford to bring out something for the family man without losing a reputation for flat-out

sportscar manufacture which was growing almost daily. Further evidence came when the prototype Marzal, which never made production, was toned down into the Urraco. Designed by Gandini in 1967 and built by Bertone, the Marzal was a gullwing four-seater with massive glazed areas in the doors extending well below the waistline. Power for this came from a straight six which was simply half of the V12 and was indicative of Lamborghini thinking.

The car which did make it into production, the pretty and successful Urraco, appeared in 1971 with conventional doors and window areas and powered by a 2.5-liter Lamborghini V8. Later versions included the Urraco S and, in 1976, the rare Targa version, the Silhouette, with thick B-pillar rollover bar very similar to Targa versions of the Porsche 911. In 1974, soon after the introduction of the Urraco, came another styling exercise by Marcello Gandini and Bertone which was based on the Urraco but featured the much flatter and sharper wedge shape which is characteristic of current production sportscars from all over the world. The Bravo was never a production car, although it represents as much of a design and styling zenith as the Miura did when it was first unveiled.

But there was already a replacement for the Miura, and this was the stunning Countach; arguably the pinnacle of Lamborghini's achievement, it was beyond any doubt a car to make Enzo Ferrari jealous of his upstart neighbor. The engine was the proven Lamborghini V12, although there was at the time some flirtation with the big 5.9-liter Chrysler V8 engines. They had appeared in the Cheetah, another open two-seater which used the American engine principally so that Lamborghini could offer his customers an automatic which financial problems prevented him developing himself. But for the production run the Countach was fitted with the high-revving V12, mounted longitudinally over the rear wheels, with the gearbox nose protruding forward between the seats.

First models had an enlarged 4.9-liter version of the V12, but later models reverted to the faithful 4-liter at the same time as the breathtaking Gandini body was placed onto a tubular chassis and given NACA ducts in the sides, air intakes on top of the rear fenders and ducts in the cockpit sides. The curves around the cut-off rear were straightened at the same time, and the later models are clearly different from the earlier 4.9-liter versions.

Power output from this was again immense, and the car was rather faster than its predecessors; the top speed was given as 190mph, the sort of speed which is only suitable for the Mulsanne straight and beyond doubt would make the Countach the fastest production

Top and right: Based around the show-only V12 Marzal, the Urraco had a 2.5-liter V8 engine, was designed by Gandini and built by Bertone.

Above: The Lambo logo.

car available, well ahead of anything Ferrari could offer. On the test track it even outperformed its drivers, with handling capabilities said to be beyond the psychological limits of the people who drovè it.

Lamborghini's financial worries looked set to see an end to the Countach as well as the rest of car production, but the company was reconstituted in 1980 as Nuova Automobili Ferruccio Lamborghini and production continued unabated; two new models, the rear-engined Jalpa V8 and a revised Cheetah – the LM 001, this time with an American Motors V8 – were introduced; the Countach continued also. In fact it is the only Lamborghini normally available overseas, and is now powered by a 5-liter aluminum version of the V12 which develops enough power to give it a top speed of 165mph. This is faster than Ferrari's current police-baiter, the 512BB, and roughly the same as the Aston Martin V8 Vantage. The prices are more or less the same as well, at a cool $70,000; if looks and performance hadn't qualified the Countach as a supercar then the sticker price would.

All pictures: The breathtaking Countach. The sort of car which other manufacturers might build as a show car is available for street use from Lamborghini.

Lincoln Continental

The Lincoln Company was founded by Henry Leland in 1917. This was the man who had rescued Henry Ford's second venture from collapse and renamed it Cadillac. When Lincoln hit financial problems in 1922 Henry snapped it up for $8 million and promptly reneged on all his promises to leave Leland in control by summarily dismissing him. Ford left the new acquisition to his son Edsel, his own attention being completely directed towards the Model T. Edsel said that while his father made the most popular car in the world, he planned to make the best.

After the Wall Street Crash Lincoln's sights were somewhat lowered, and their products owed more to Ford than to any other influence. Then the Briggs coachbuilding firm produced a car designed by Tom Tjaarda; Edsel saw it as a new small Lincoln, and after revision to accept a new V12 engine, the Lincoln-Zephyr was born. It was on this successful base that Edsel decided to have a personal car built for himself in 1938. He got Bob Gregorie, whom he had appointed head of the styling department he had created in 1932, to handle the styling for him, but his major instruction was to 'make it as continental as possible.'

Gregorie complied, but it was Edsel who insisted that an externally-mounted spare wheel in a special carrier was an essential part of 'being continental.' This one-off for Edsel incorporated a 12-inch stretched Zephyr hood and chopped-down Zephyr doors on the specially-built chassis. The rest of the body was handmade to Gregorie's 1/10-scale clay model. The result was an elegant, well-balanced shape which was destined to be a classic, despite the fact that it had simply been handbuilt to fulfill one man's dreams.

Lincoln power was standardized on the 266ci L-head V12 introduced for the Zephyr, which at the beginning produced some 110hp at about 3600rpm. It also gave maximum torque at an incredible 400rpm, making it almost strong enough to scale vertical walls and making the gearbox virtually redundant. Unbelievably there was also an overdrive on the three-speed gearbox, operated from a knob on the steering wheel and effective over about 20mph.

By the time Edsel's personal car was finished the V12 was giving an improved 120hp, and with this sort of power on tap he set off on his annual pilgrimage to Palm Beach. He returned with over 200 orders for the car, which was now called the Lincoln Continental.

Edsel was so pleased with the car that he had already ordered two more for his sons, Henry II and Benson. Now, however, it went into production as a handbuilt item in order to build a limited quantity of 500, for the 200 who had seen the car at Palm Beach and those other of Edsel's friends and contemporaries who could afford it. By late 1939 only 25 had been made, but in 1940 – in the slightly shorter Zephyr sheet metal for the model year – 404 Continentals were made, 54 coupés and the rest cabriolet versions.

In 1941, with only minor detail changes, the Continental really caught on; America liked it, to the extent of 400 cabriolets and 800 coupés (the only two body styles available) in the model year. Perhaps in 1942 the Continental would have sold even better, though the styling changes which squared up its appearance now made it look rather heavier and more cumbersome than Edsel's original. In fact it was about six inches longer, and most of that was overhanging chrome – the new bumpers were much bigger than before, and the almost delicately scalloped grille on the original had given way to a more traditional but heavyweight arrangement. Engine capacity went up to 292ci, taking the power up to 130hp.

But only 336 Continentals were made; 1942 was the year the United States entered World War II, and the factories were turned over to the production of war

matériel – the very thing Leland's original Lincoln Company had been formed to do and the cessation of which, in 1918, had brought him to Henry Ford's doorstep. In this conflict, though, it was the Ford empire which churned out a huge quantity of vital supplies – at one time the Willow Run Plant made a complete Liberator bomber every hour.

In 1943 Edsel Ford died; he had taken over from his father in 1941 after an ugly power struggle which ended when Henry Ford suffered a stroke. After Edsel's death an 80-year-old Henry resumed his post as President and Chief Executive, but he abdicated in favour of Henry II in 1945 and it was left to his grandson to resurrect the car-making capacity when the war was over. Like the products of practically every other American auto maker, the 1946 Fords were little more than revitalised 1942 models – and that included the Continental. Both prewar models went on sale once more in January, the cabriolet now termed a convertible coupé, at fractionally over $4000 – little more than they had cost in 1942.

Still powered by the V12 mounted in the same standard 125-inch wheelbase and devoid of most of the vulgar brightwork of the time, they simply bore their name in script lettering on the hood. The most noticeable change which distinguished the prewar Continental from the rushed-into-the-showroom 1946 model was the thick-barred eggcrate grille. The first full year after the end of hostilities saw a total of 446 almost evenly split between coupés and convertibles. In 1947 the Continental enjoyed its most successful sales year as another almost even split of coupés and convertibles ran to 1569 units. Sales were nearly as good for the unchanged 1948 cars, but this time sales of the 1299 cars were heavily biased in favour of what were now called club coupés – nobody wanted the convertibles.

Production of the $5000 car was halted before the end of the year as Ford's energies were concentrated once again on low-price volume production; at the time Ford boasted only one car in their entire range which cost more than $2000. There was little room for the anachronistic handbuilt Continental in the bustle of the postwar boom, and in any case the man who had seen his own dream turn into a production reality was no longer there to protect it. With shorter wheelbases and cars which were altogether more practical Lincoln enjoyed poor-to-middling fortunes through the next decade and only in 1961, when the company produced a car of such elegant styling that the design team won an industry award, was the Continental name, now indelibly established as belonging to a marque of superlative style and excellence, once more affixed to a Lincoln hood.

Below: A Continental from 1941, the year Edsel Ford's personal dream car began to sell well.

Bottom: The 1948 model, with somewhat altered sheet metal. This was to be the last year of the handbuilt Continentals.

Maserati

Alfieri Maserati was, like so many car makers before him and after him, a racing driver before he and his brother Ernesto decided in 1926 to form their own company and build their own vehicles. Their ambitions lay in the direction of motorsport, and they were almost immediately successful. Entering the highest planes of circuit racing, they scooped no less than five Grand Prix wins in 1930, their first full season of competition, establishing an instant identity which few makers can equal. When the company was taken over by Count Orsi in 1937 he too concentrated on racing, although there were occasional handbuilt road cars available.

For Maserati, the production of road cars in any volume began with the 3500GT in 1958, following up Fangio's success of the previous year when he had become World Champion at the wheel of a Maserati and given the company the Constructors' title as well.

The 3500GT was bodied by a wide assortment of specialist builders which included Vignale, Frua, Ghia, Bertone and, mostly, Milan-based Touring.

Even then, Maserati have hardly been involved in anything like mass production, building their range of exotic sports/touring machinery in small numbers and with great care. With their Italian counterparts at Ferrari and Lamborghini, the influence of these sportscars on the motoring world has always been out of all proportion to their number. And, while their products have no real relationship with the kind of motoring most people are obliged to perform, it is by those same people that the Italian sportscars are hailed as 'real' cars which, they say, Detroit would do well to observe and copy. However, all that is without regard to the totally impractical nature of the handmade thoroughbred.

For example, the stock Maserati engine which had powered their racing program was used in a more powerful version of the straight-six 3500GT. Designated 5000GT, it was handmade, extremely expensive to buy and even more costly to run, using 5-liter race engines with dual overhead camshafts and 330hp on tap. The first customer was the Shah of Iran.

As the road cars progressed in popularity so the range expanded, although the basic engineering tended to stay the same. The GT series led to the Mistrale, then the Quattroporte and then the first of a line of Maseratis which were far more than simply exotic.

Styled by Ghia and based on the previous year's Mexico, the two-seat Ghibli appeared at the Turin show in 1966. The Mexico had suffered at the hands of Ferrari and then the newly-arrived Lamborghini and Iso, and the stunning new Ghia design was the Maserati

Above left: A British-registered example of the expensive and speedy Bora.

Below: The Khamsin, styled by Bertone and introduced to the Maserati range in 1972.

All pictures: This spyder version was part of the 1200 production units reached by the Ghibli. Its strong chassis construction enabled the soft-top to be made relatively easily.

response. Powered by the same basic quad-cam V8, at 4.1 or 4.9 liters, the Ghibli used the same steel hull bolted onto a tubular and box-section chassis, with independent coil-and-wishbone front suspension and a live rear axle.

The Ghibli was a fine car and attracted a great deal of attention and – for the market – lots of customers. More than 1200 were built in its six-year life, and in the end it was the fuel crisis not the competition which closed it off. The Indy was in production shortly after the Ghibli, and lasted two years longer. Basically a derivative of the same series, the Vignale-styled Indy was one of the new 2+2 layout cars, and was the first Maserati to use monocoque construction, which meant that there could be no one-offs or convertibles for wealthy oriental potentates. But the Indy was fast, with a top end around 160mph for ZF manuals and a little over 140mph for the automatics; 60mph came up in about seven seconds, the standing quarter in fifteen.

The Indy sold well, making more than 1100 units up to 1976 when it was axed as part of a rationalization program instituted when the company was sold off. But by then Maserati had been forced to move with the times. Ferrari had established that the mid-engined layout was to be the one which every manufacturer of

supercars would have to follow and Giulio Alfieri, one of the few survivors remaining from the Orsi racing days after Citroen took over, designed the Bora accordingly. Styled by Giugiaro, it had the 330hp light-alloy V8 lengthways ahead of the rear wheels, four-wheel coilover independent suspension and a claimed top speed approaching 170mph. This was widely held to be somewhat optimistic, and 160mph would be a more realistic figure.

In ride and handling the Bora was typical of its class – although defining its class simply as 'supercar' is rather vague, especially since it was about 30 percent more expensive than its counterparts. The Citroen influence was particularly evident in the use of high-pressure hydraulics to power the brakes, tilt the seat squab (the seat itself had no fore-and-aft adjustment) and adjust the pedals, which slid backward and forward at the press of a dashboard button.

The Bora was joined by the Merak, which was virtually identical except that it made use of the incredibly compact V6 unit Maserati had designed for the Citroen SM. Using this, which produced a respectable 190 (later upped to 220)hp, gave enough room to redesign the rear quarters and give the Merak two very occasional rear seats.

Below: The Bora was the Giugiaro-styled follow-up to the Ghibli, and was Maserati's venture into the monocoque/mid-mounted V8 layout pioneered by Ferrari.

Inset right: The Bora's rear-mounted 330hp light-alloy V8 was mounted lengthways ahead of the rear wheels.

Introduced in 1972, the Khamsin was the only front-engine rear-drive Maserati to survive the period of Citroen ownership; it also had the distinction of being styled by Bertone. Essentially a replacement for the Indy, it used the same basic V8 powerplant and virtually identical running gear, although the live rear axle was replaced by a coil-and-wishbone setup.

Although cargo space was generous thanks to a large platform beneath the tailgate, rear passengers were doomed to discomfort. Like all Maseratis the suspension was uncompromisingly hard and there was little in the way of legroom. Headroom too was virtually non-existent, Bertone having taken the 'fastback' classification to literal extremes.

The Khamsin's styling, though, was immensely successful, since it was the first conventional-layout Maserati to attain the eyecatching sleekness which is an implicit factor of the mid-engine cars.

The Khamsin stayed as a production vehicle, although Citroen abandoned Italy after the proposed Fiat link-up fell through, and it was left to Alessandro de Tomaso – with the help of government financing – to prop up Maserati, allowing them to fit Maserati engine, transmission and badgework to the big four-seat Longchamps and call it the Maserati Kyalami.

Mercedes Benz

Gottlieb Daimler produced what was probably the first successful four-wheel car in the world, based on a horse-drawn carriage, in 1886, and immediately began supplying his vehicles to those wealthy enough to afford them.

Locksmith Karl Benz was a little slower; by 1884 his two-stroke engine – using coil ignition rather than the hot-tube type – was running well; his four-stroke followed soon afterwards, and he began selling motor tricycles in 1886. A four-wheeler appeared in 1892, but despite his willingness to devise or adopt new solutions it took the spur of race competition against his rival, Daimler – by now racing his cars under the Mercedes badge – to make him see the advantages of things like pneumatic tyres.

After the 1914-18 War, as the German economy wallowed in a depression soon to afflict others, talks of a merger between Daimler and Benz first began, but the amalgamation didn't finally take place until 1926.

The Daimler-Benz quest for engineering excellence through racetrack development and success continued through the late twenties and into the thirties. It led to intensive and successful research with superchargers and into the production of some of the most classically elegant roadsters of the period. The supercharging

development was carried into the Grand Prix racing of the thirties and the Mercedes name began to appear more and more frequently in the record books. The 1935 season was dominated by the 430hp W25, but two years later the W125 arrived, packing a stupendous 650hp and capable of 200mph. Later the trend was for smaller cars, and Mercedes kept their top speeds as high as their enormous predecessors with better streamlining and higher supercharger boost.

The engineer behind much of this development work is better known for the cars bearing his own name which went into production after World War II; Ferdinand Porsche's expertise was the key to the success of cars like the legendary 1928 Mercedes SSK, which developed 225hp from its 7.1-liter engine. The designation of the cars revolved partly around the new blown engines; there was the 6.8-liter S – or Sports – Mercedes, followed soon after by the bigger 7.1 Super Sports. The K referred to the chassis, based on the luxury touring models supplied by Daimler-Benz but somewhat shortened (hence *kurz*, or short) for better handling qualities.

Built to the expected high standards, these rakish vehicles were favorites among the stars of the burgeoning film industry, and were often fitted with

Top: The 4½ litre race car that won the French Grand Prix for Mercedes in 1914.

Left and above right: The famous Mercedes SSK, the 7.1 litre Super Sports model of 1928 with a shortened chassis for improved handling.

special bodywork; Al Jolson had his own boat-tail SSK built in 1928. But despite their glossy image, they weren't just fast and good-looking sports tourers. These were also very strong, successful working cars.

These were the competition cars raced so successfully by the likes of Rudi Caracciola in Grand Prix, Formula Libre, in the Le Mans 24 Hours – where he became involved in a memorable dogfight with Sir Henry 'Tim' Birkin and the Bentley Boys (which they won) in 1930 – at Belfast, where he scored his famous wet-weather victory in the TT against strong opposition from the blower Bentleys, and his epic victory in the 1931 Mille Miglia.

Away from the track, Caracciola had his own Mercedes – yet another classic of the period, a 5-liter supercharged Limousine Coupé designated the 500K. In convertible form this was perhaps the best-looking full-fendered sportscar ever made, designed in the true thirties idiom; in retrospect, it stands against any car built before or since as a pinnacle of achievement, a

Above: The distinctive shape of the gullwing 300SL hardtop.

Left: The 300SL in less spectacular convertible form.

Above right: The pre-war 540K, seen here as a Sindlefingen Custom Cabriolet A.

Right: A 1934 500K Limousine Coupé owned by Mercedes' race driver Rudi Caracciola and possibly the best-looking full-fendered sportscar ever made.

perfect blend of form and functionality. Its successor was the 5.4 liter 540K, also supercharged and good for about 160hp from its six cylinders.

Postwar engines were even more efficient; although Mercedes had dominated Grand Prix racing right through the thirties, there was still room for improvement, and the race engines of the fifties developed more than twice the power of the big blown prewar units. It was this much-improved power-to-weight ratio which lay behind the success of Mercedes' return to the top in racing, with the 300SL – Sports Light – on which a whole series of Mercedes sportscars, from the 190SL

onwards, were based. A brief and total domination of road racing in the early fifties ended after Levegh's horrific accident at the 1955 Le Mans with the 300SLR, a car based on the W196 GP car rather than the 300SL.

Had this development continued there would, perhaps, be a stablemate for the excellent 500SL. Although its engineering now bears little, if any, reference to those first postwar sportscars, it still has the visual hallmark of its heritage, and the parameters which made the 300SL what it was still apply to the 500SL – extreme tractability, tremendous power, opulent luxury and superb engineering.

Above: A 1979 Mercedes 450SEL and (*right*) the interior of a similar car.

Below: The suffix of this stylish 500SEL Coupé stands for Energy Concept, Mercedes' stated intention being 'to make cars less demanding of the world's dwindling fuel supplies.'

Panther

The original Panther Westwinds company has long since vanished, but the marque survives thanks to the intervention and direction of Korean businessman and enthusiast Young Kim.

Prior to that the company had been little more than the hobby of Robert Jankel, a sometime engine tuner who had switched professions and gone into the textile business. It had been so profitable that he had been able to design and built his own one-off specials, averagely about one each year. He had just built a thirties look-alike which was, in appearance at least, strongly reminiscent of the Jaguar SS100. Continuing the association, it used a box-section chassis very similar to that of the SS, and the power was by a Jaguar straight six.

In 1971 Jankel sold his textile interests and con-centrated instead on putting his latest creation – which he'd named the Panther, again invoking memories of the Big Cat – into regular (if not actually series) production. Gradually, as demand for his elegant car grew, production grew to meet it and the company expanded into its own factory, absorbing some of the smaller specialist concerns who had previously worked for them. Although they did subcontract work for an assortment of clients – including Rolls-Royce – it was the excellence of the Panther J72, as it now is, on which the company was founded.

The 4.2-liter Jaguar engine sat above a tubular-beam axle and fed power through an E-type gearbox to a coil-sprung rear axle. At the front, Jankel used Formula One-style coilover units. The body was

Above: The superb Panther De Ville perfectly captured the flavor of the luxury limousines of the thirties.

Below: The J72 was, at £52,000, the cheap end of the Panther replicar range. Built to order, it used Jaguar components and duplicated the 'feel', if not the exact looks, of the SS100.

aluminum and finished to an extremely high standard, matching the workmanship of the interior. The Panther had a genuine, handcrafted period feel, but it handled and drove more like a modern car; with its four-wheel disk brakes, it stopped like one too.

The J72 in production was a low-volume item; Panther made two, sometimes three cars a week. They also ran up a few styling exercises like the Lazer, and even did some specials on the J72 body.

For people with even greater sums of money to spend the J72 could be moved upmarket, for example with the installation of a 5.3-liter Jaguar V12. Although it had most of the aerodynamic qualities of a sticky brick the Panther weighed little, and the V12 could boost it to about 140mph quite quickly, hitting 60mph in 5.7 seconds and 100 in 14, covering the standing quarter in about the same time. The same applied to the Panther FF, which forsook Jaguar mechanicals in favour of Ferrari. This was also blindingly fast, a fact which will shock nobody.

The J72 was soon followed by the more reasonably-priced Lima, another full-fendered open two-seater which evoked the spirit of the thirties without actually qualifying as a replica. This was based on Vauxhall components, but was met with a mixed reaction. Although Vauxhall is the British arm of GM it was not a terrifically popular make at the time, and was probably not the best base for a car of this nature.

There was also the eyecatching Batmobile lookalike, the Panther Six – or rather there were two of them. Six-wheelers, with two sets of front wheels, these were dramatic looking and dramatic in price. One of them is now believed to be in the Middle East, while the other remains in Britain where Chameleon Cars of London's Park Lane offered it, complete with onboard computer, for a reputed £100,000. Once again the standard of workmanship was to an exceedingly high level, but even as a styling exercise it was rather more of a curiosity than a car.

Then Panther Westwinds got into financial difficulties, and it looked as if they might cease operations altogether until Young Kim stepped into the picture. Since his arrival the company has undergone a certain amount of what Detroit would call 'rationalization,' and the future is looking extremely bright indeed.

Below and right: The De Ville was available as a hardtop or a convertible, and featured a horseshoe radiator not entirely dissimilar to that which typified the thirties' Bugattis.

Above and left: The Panther Six was, if nothing else, eyecatching. Only two were built; one is in the Middle East, the other was on sale in London recently for an astronomical asking price.

John Canvin came to Panther from Peugeot, and as his first task brought the Lima up to date; it now continues as the Kallista. But the most significant work at their Byfleet factory has been the emergence of a new sportscar. Young Kim felt that the company needed something more modern and easier to build than the Kallista, and that there was a gap in the sportscar market left after the demise of the TR7 and the MGB, so the company began to look at a two-seater which would carry a sticker price below £10,000 and which could be produced at the rate of up to 2000 units a year.

Enter Ken Greenley and John Heffernan, who both worked for GM design, to take care of styling; enter also Len Bailey, a chassis designer of considerable repute. Bailey worked on Ford's GT 40 and the later C100, the Le Mans-winning Gulf Mirage of Ickx and Bell and a host of other projects as well. Between them, they created a mid-engined two-seater with a very Group C-style chassis which places the driver and passenger right forward in the car and the transverse Ford 1600 engine ahead of the rear wheels without creating an overcramped cockpit. Race enthusiast Bailey wanted a more powerful engine; the chassis is designed to cope with a great deal more than the injected Ford's quoted 105hp, and in reality he was looking ahead to a four-wheel-drive version of the new car, launched at the 1984 British Motor Show as the Panther Solo.

Whether or not this will enter production remains to be seen; if it does it could cost anything up to £45,000, a price completely at odds with the original design aims and sales philosophy.

What is more definite is that the Solo will get more power, either from Ford's turbo version of the 1600 unit or from an alternative source, perhaps a twin-cam Toyota or the Douvrin V6 which is currently in everything from Renaults to Volvos.

In any event, the Panther Solo looks all set to do what the big giants can't; fill the need for a specialist two-seater at a price which is well below the £25,000 super-car bracket occupied by Ferrari, Porsche, Corvette *et al.* If it does then it will get its own status, and deservedly so. Morgan have proved that small car makers can survive very well if they fulfill a particular need, and that building nostalgia is far from being the easiest path to financial success. Many companies have tried to market the kind of car Panther have just designed; only Lotus has stayed the course, eventually with help from Toyota. The future of the Byfleet sportster is sure to be interesting, even if it's far from certain. It remains to be seen whether Young Kim can do what John De Lorean couldn't.

Porsche 911

On 30 June 1984 a showroom stock Porsche 930 (more commonly known simply as a 911 Turbo) won the title of the world's fastest-accelerating production sportscar in a time trial held on an old English airfield. A Lamborghini Countach placed second, an Aston Martin V8 Vantage third and a Lotus Esprit turbo was fourth; sadly there was no Ferrari in evidence, since the competition was for current production vehicles only – the BBi had finished and the new GTO and Testa Rossa were not then in production.

Even the new GTO would have to try hard to beat the Porsche's undramatic performance; the Countach smoked off the line and a considerable distance down the strip, but an appealing power squat was the only evidence of the Porsche flat-six 3.3's 300hp rushing it to a 23.9-second, 135mph standing kilometer.

The turbo story began in postwar Germany when Ferdinand Porsche was already 72 years old. His work for Daimler, Mercedes-Benz, Steyr, NSU and Auto-Union, not to mention the ubiquitous VW Beetle, had gained him a legendary reputation as an automotive genius. His interests lay directly – and exclusively - in sports racing cars. He had talked the Hitler government into funding a racing team of three cars in the thirties and as soon as the war ended he re-established the Porsche design company – which had been set up in April 1931 – in Austria; the first automobile to bear the Porsche name made its debut two years later, in 1948. He lived just long enough to see the company's first serious race car – the VW-based 356, designed by his son – win its class at Le Mans in 1951 (in the hands of one Zora Arkus Duntov) before succumbing to a stroke the following year.

His son Ferry took over and continued the great man's work and ideals; Porsche have never produced anything bearing their badge that wasn't a fast, exciting, reliable and brilliantly engineered sportscar. The rear-mounted boxer configuration of that first 356 has been retained right up to the present day, although its capacity is now rather greater than the original 1131cc flat four, which was upped to 60hp after considerable cylinder-head modification.

The first roadgoing Porsche was the Speedster, based on a development of the first 356, but minus spaceframe chassis; it had the traditional VW platform chassis with torsion-bar suspension, independent all

The 356 coupé (top right) and convertible (top far right) were the first roadgoing cars to bear the Porsche name. Although the design criteria have remained the same the result is rather different, exemplified by the 1985 930 Turbo (far right).

round. It grew into a four-cam two-liter after racetrack experience which had given the little cars success at Le Mans and Ferrari a fright. But the development through the next stage took the Speedster into its third generation and was fittingly the work of the third generation of the Porsche family to be involved. It was Ferry's son Ferdinand who did most of the work as the curves of the 356 were trimmed away and flattened and the window area enlarged. The new engine was Ferdinand's work, a single-cam flat six of two liters largely based on the eight-cylinder race engine. With engine and transmission slung out over the rear wheels – some might say too far aft for comfort and peace of mind – long before the mid-engined configuration became mandatory in the supercar league, extensive use was made of weight-saving aluminum for the individual cylinders and a strong crankcase to hold the forged-steel crankshaft.

It was originally designated the Porsche 901, but by the middle of 1964, when it went into production alongside the 356, it had been renamed the 911. Discontinuing the 356 in 1965 left Porsche without a convertible in their lineup, and the 911 Targa followed quickly. The 130hp engine was uprated for the 1966 911S – which ran 160hp – but the real power came from racetrack development, where winning experience led to the 2300cc unit which was soon fitted with fuel injection. The 2300 911E (*Einspritz* is the German designation for injection) was soon on the roads, followed by 500 lightweight homologation specials powered by a 2700cc motor and classified as Carreras. This was so successful that the lesser powerplants were dropped in its favour and the 2.7-liter unit became standard throughout the Porsche lineup – with one exception. Yet another racebred special, the Carrera RSR was given a 3-liter engine which poked out an astounding 200hp and was apparently the ultimate development of the 911 series.

Not so: later in the same year there was another step forward which was so dramatic it was officially classified completely differently, although almost everyone outside of Stuttgart refused to recognise its 930 designation. Basically a turbocharged Carrera RSR, years of development had gone into the KKK turbo to deliver a matchless refinement of power. Clutch and transmission had to be considerably strengthened to cope with the 300hp now being developed by this 193-inch

Below and right: The SC version is the 'standard' Porsche 911, if any such thing exists. With 230hp out of 3.2 liters, its quoted top speed is fractionally above 150mph.

Left and below left: The Carrera, once the slightly more powerful 911 version, has now replaced the old 911SC entirely.

flat six. The 930 ran from 0-60 in 5.3 seconds, passed the standing quarter in 13.4 and kept right on to a top speed of 160mph. Along the way it kept two adults in luxury in the front and two in comparatively cramped comfort in the back.

The three-liter unit which was the basis of the turbo became 3.3 liters, while the normally-aspirated engines are now 3.2 liters. Even without the benefits provided by the KKK turbo the 911SC kicks out a staggering 231hp, blasts past 60mph in six seconds and has a top

speed of 152mph. It's so close to the turbo top end that the presence of the electronic rev limiter is clearly evident. The 930 is one of the most successful sports racing cars ever available for street use, and in its track-only format – like the Kremer 935 – it is hugely successful in a variety of classes, particularly long-distance endurance racing. Watching the 930 perform at Le Mans or somewhere similar makes it obvious that once the engine is free to rev beyond 7000rpm it is easily capable of a great deal more than 160mph.

Right: The 1976 Carrera 3-liter in Targa form with a silver rollover bar.

Below: The matt black rollover bar of the 1981 Targa 911 now plays down the once-distinctive feature.

Porsche 928S

Initial design work on the eventual replacement for the 911 was begun in the early seventies at the same time as Volkswagen were asking Porsche for a car to replace their 914, which was to have a family resemblance to Porsche. Consequently the 924 was developed alongside the 928, although the 924 was eventually released as a Porsche after VW backed out.

The decision to abandon the rear-engine layout which had lasted for so long was prompted by a number of factors. Aside from the question of usable interior space, which is at a minimum, the rear-engine configuration presents major noise problems. All the principal sources of noise are grouped together in the same place and aircooled engines, particularly alloy ones, are noisy anyway. The water jacket absorbs much of the mechanical noise produced in an engine, a major factor in helping it to meet international regulations.

At the same time it seemed advisable to make the engine somewhat larger than the aircooled variety in the 911; lower engine revs make less noise but still produce power, and in any case it would have to be capable of absorbing emission control regulations which might sap the power of a small-capacity powerplant. That such a large engine would have to be front-mounted was clear; the handling problems it would present at the rear were unthinkable, and having it at the front would help the car meet the increasingly severe impact requirements. To help the new car achieve a better driving balance a transaxle was mounted inside the wheelbase just ahead of the rear axle. (On the cheaper 924 cost-saving and use of available parts put the transaxle behind the rear axle.)

To keep the hood line as low as possible while packing a suitably large powerplant meant that the new engine would have to be V-shaped and the eventual production engine was a 4.4-liter dohc V8 with Bosch fuel injection and 240hp. Within the V8 were hydraulic lifters and aluminum pistons, and a special casting process was developed to make an aluminum block which was silicon-lined. Greater reliability and longer life were two benefits, and the closer tolerances between piston and cylinder walls which was the primary objective produced more power, less noise and better fuel economy thanks to improved combustion and a lower loss of combustion gases – in other words better efficiency from thoughtful engineering, which has always been the Porsche hallmark.

The torque-tube drive fed a light-action double-plate clutch or the automatic transmission torque converter; at its introduction five-speed manual was the standard transmission, with Daimler-Benz automatic as an option. Only later, as automatics outsold manuals three

Right and below right: The 928S (pictured) was always more popular than the straight 928.

Below: The original Porsches were race cars, and although the 911 is still a reasonably rare competition vehicle it's more frequently seen than a 924 like the one pictured.

to one, would the situation reverse. By the time the 928S Series 2 emerged for 1984 the most popular alternative to three-speed auto was the new four-speed transmission which Porsche recommend as standard. Although it is marginally slower than the manual at 155mph, and has slightly higher fuel consumption at cruising speed, it is far smoother as a high-speed tourer, which is what it is intended to be.

Wishbone suspension front and rear was based on experience gained from the highly successful sports racing cars from 904 through 936 mostly because of their ultimate superiority over strut or torsion-bar types, and extensive use was made of aluminum in their construction to save weight. The 'Weissach' trailing-arm setup used at the rear was developed first for the 914 and 'steers' the rear wheels to toe-in when slowing down; conventional trailing-arm systems produce unstable toe-out. Rack-and-pinion steering is powered by ZF and reduces servo input as engine speed rises, giving high assistance for parking and correct response with on-center feel at high speeds.

The steel body features an integral rollover bar and aluminum panels for doors, hood and front fenders and moulded nosecone and tail concealing the bumpers. The plastic is 'self-healing' and covered with elasticated paint which springs in and out of shape without cracking. Inside, the whole instrument panel moves with the tilt steering wheel and the pedals are adjustable. Door mirrors are electrically heated and adjustable and the

airconditioning extends as far as the glovebox, presumably to keep candy or drinks cool as well as people.

In 1978 the 928 became European Car of the Year, but by 1980 there was also the rather more appealing 928S, with engine capacity upped to 4.6 liters. This gave 25 percent more power, and the chassis had been uprated to match it. Externally the only visible signs were the vestigial rear spoiler and slotted alloy wheels, but by 1982 the popularity of the S over the stock 928 was such that the soft option was unobtrusively phased out. Then in 1984 came the Series 2. Other than the new four-speed automatic transmission and the introduction of electronically-sensed ABS anti-lock braking, changes were mostly of a minor nature and centered around increases in power and torque to give 310hp at 5900rpm from the larger capacity and raised compression ratio (up from 8.5:1 to 10:1). With this extra power on tap the electronic rev limiter was shifted up from 6200 to 6500rpm, although press road testers seemed to find that only the manual could make any real use of the extra rpm. Its top speed was now in the region of 158mph, although the automatic had trouble getting above 150 through its new four-speed, which suffers from fairly large amounts of converter slip, also making surprisingly large amounts of throttle necessary for small bursts of acceleration at lower speeds. Conversely the 928 steps off the line from a standing start very smartly indeed, with a 0-60 of 6.5 seconds and 0-100 in 16.3 – no less than might be expected from a car which costs around $30,000.

The price isn't a great deal different to the red-blooded 911 turbo, and performance – though not quite as shattering – is reasonably similar. The difference is that the 928S is a blue-blooded tourer rather than a race car for the street.

Left: 1982 was the last year for the stock 928, before it was phased out and the more powerful 928S (*above and right*), distinguished by a few external features such as its rear spoiler, was left to continue alone.

Rolls-Royce Silver Ghost

Henry Royce was a miller's son who became obsessed with engineering. He built his first car in 1903 at his engineering factory in Cooke Street, Manchester, largely because he found the cars available to him to be unsatisfactory.

The Hon Charles Rolls was a motoring enthusiast, putting up the best performance in the 1900 Thousand Miles Trial, the event which brought motorsport to the attention of the British public for the first time. He had an agency in London, selling Minerva and Panhard et Levassor cars.

In 1904 Henry Royce demonstrated his car to C S Rolls; their first partnership agreement was dated 23 December the same year, and from then on it is safe to say that neither of them had any cause to look back with anything except complete satisfaction.

Two years later their business agreement became even firmer, and Rolls-Royce Limited was registered in March 1906 with a share capital of £60,000. New premises were sought to build bigger cars in greater volume, and the company moved to Derby. Rolls continued to promote the sales of the cars by means of extremely active participation in all forms of motorsport. His own tenacity, coupled with the mechanical excellence and sheer staying power of the cars, soon won the kind of acclaim the company needed.

In 1906 what is arguably one of the most famous motorcars ever was first built. The fabled Silver Ghost ran non-stop from London to Edinburgh and back, in third gear all the way, and was then run continuously, day and night, for a further 15,000 miles.

The 40/50 that followed was advertised as 'the best six-cylinder car in the world,' just as the 30hp had been advertised the previous year as 'the best car in the world.' According to Rolls-Royce it was the most graceful, attractive, silent, flexible, reliable and smooth-running six-cylinder car yet produced.

Royce's uncompromising engineering standards

were well known long before he made his first car, but they were to become a legend. He once said 'It is impossible for us to make a bad car. The doorman wouldn't let it go out.'

That kind of reputation began with cars like the supremely elegant Silver Ghost, and was derived from Royce's persistent ability to find intelligent engineering solutions to long-standing problems. In this case it was the heart of the Ghost's two banks of three cylinders, the crankshaft, of which Royce – and Rolls-Royce Ltd – were most proud. Contemporary engine technology, which used white-metal crankshaft bearings, forced the use of long, thin crankshafts which were virtually flexible; the bearings would melt quite quickly if sustained high revs were applied, further restricting the engine's efficiency. Royce solved the problem fairly simply by providing pressurized oil feed to the bearings; up until that point all crankshafts had been splash-lubricated.

Above and left: One of a handful of cars which is instantly recognizable to just about everybody, the original Silver Ghost dates from the days before the Spirit of Ecstasy mascot was created for Rolls-Royce.

This, together with crankshaft design and dimensions which are virtually the same as modern items but were then completely new, was the core of the Silver Ghost's reliable powerplant. The company considered it such an important advance and so crucial to their superiority over other engine builders that at the Olympia Motor Show the car was shown with the oil pan removed and a mirror placed underneath to aid inspection of the crank.

With refinements to engine construction, ignition and induction systems, the 3.2:1 compression ratio gave the 7428cc engine 48bhp at 1250rpm. The model which made the historic London-Edinburgh-London run had a compression ratio of 3.5:1 and a bigger carburetor, which allowed it a massive 58hp and a top speed of 78mph. But it was not an engine designed for high revs, and gave maximum torque from about 200rpm, making every gear but top virtually redundant – which is why the marathon run was easily accomplished in third gear. In those days there was definitely no such thing as synchromesh, and changing gear in any car was a noisy operation calling for considerable strength of mind as well as limb. Any car which could manage to deal with most situations in top gear was thus far more desirable than one in which frequent changes were a necessity. The Silver Ghost could encompass a full range of driving between 5 and 38mph in top.

One model out of the pre-production run was set aside to be the promotional vehicle which would establish the 40/50 in the public eye. Finished in aluminum paint and with silver-plated fittings, it was named the Silver Ghost; the name stuck, being applied to the entire 40/50 sidevalve range.

In 1910 Royce, who was a chronic workaholic, collapsed and from then on conducted the running of the company from his residence in France by mail. In the

same year Rolls, who had just become the first Englishman to fly the English Channel and the first person to make the round trip non-stop, took off from Bournemouth in his Wright Flyer, now modified to a French design by the Short brothers. The Rolls-Royce chief engineer was not happy about the new design, and his fears were well-founded; Charles Rolls died when it crashed on landing.

The Silver Ghost continued in production at Derby right up until 1925, a total of 6173 being built. The cars were initially sold as an engine/chassis combination, and Rolls-Royce 'invited' customers to fit them with tires, body and accessories from any manufacturer of their choice, although they declined to accept responsibility for anything which was not of their workmanship. Landaulettes, Limousines, Broughams and Roi des Belges were among the variety of body styles available, although there was a much longer list. Coachbuilding firms like Lawtons and Barker and Hooper supplied bodies as elegant as those names might suggest, and there were a number of far more exotic constructions – a wooden boat-tail was even applied to a 1914 chassis by Schebera-Shapiro of Berlin.

But it was that very first silver Silver Ghost which remained the most famous, even though its radiator shell was crowned with an AA badge, not the now-famous Spirit of Ecstasy mascot. Sculptor Charles Sykes created that in 1911 and the first Rolls-Royce graced by its presence was the 40/50 Silver Ghost.

Above: Rear view of Rolls-Royce's most famous car, the original Silver Ghost.

Right: The Roi des Belges body was one of many different styles available from coachbuilders on the Silver Ghost chassis.

Rolls-Royce America

A bare six months after the signing of that historic contract between Charles Rolls and Henry Royce the export drive began: by September of 1906 Charles Rolls was on his way to the United States, taking with him three cars as examples of the company's wares. One of them was sold almost as soon as it was unloaded from the ship and went straight away to Texas. Of the remaining two, one was kept on the road as a demonstration model, while by December of that year the other had been put on display in the New York Auto Show, later to become the place where a wide range of now-famous cars would make their debuts. That first appearance at the show was a success for Rolls-Royce too; four orders were taken for new cars and an American distributor was appointed: W C Martin of New York City.

In 1907 there were another 17 orders for new Rolls-Royce cars, the bulk of them sparked off simply because the doyenne of New York society, Mrs Astor, had ordered one for herself. Shortly before the outbreak of the war in 1914 Rolls-Royce appointed a new American distributor, the established – and distinguished – Brewster coachbuilding firm. In less than 12 months before the outbreak of hostilites they proved

themselves more than able, selling slightly in excess of 100 vehicles.

In 1919, though, Rolls-Royce once again turned their exporting ambitions towards the United States; the company believed that the potential market there was far bigger than anything they could hope to achieve in Britain. So when import restrictions meant that selling British-built cars there was not going to be profitable they set about creating an American assembly facility as quickly as possible. A factory was purchased from the Springfield Wire Wheel Company at Springfield, Mass, and manufacturing was commenced at once under the guidance of Henry Royce himself. Although the workforce was recruited locally it was supplemented by the arrival of more than 50 skilled foremen, supervisors and craftsmen from the Rolls-Royce factory at Derby who had emigrated there permanently with their families.

Production at Springfield commenced in early 1921, and Rolls-Royce announced that the products of their American plant would be the equal of anything built in Derby. The plan was that parts would be shipped and assembled in the US with custom-built coachwork made by the existing – and prestigious – American

Above: An immaculately maintained Springfield Silver Ghost Pall Mall tourer dating from 1922.

Left: A 1921-vintage Silver Ghost Albany dual cowl Phaeton.

Above: One of the best-looking of the Brewster bodies was the Newmarket, seen here as a convertible on a Phantom II chassis. This vehicle dates from 1931.

Rolls-Royce Postwar

In the early days of the industry there were people who built cars; they were engineers. The people whose industry was threatened by the arrival of the motorcar – originally the horseless carriage, remember – were those who built coaches. For most engineers fine woodwork, veneer and varnishing, padding and covering seats were all things outside the scope of the machine-shop – and steel bodywork was still a thing of the future. So the coachmakers carried on coachmaking, for the car builders, and a separate industry of skilled craftsmen appeared in the form of the specialist coachbuilders.

Their boom was shortlived; the steel body was becoming more and more commonplace and the forced pace of technical advance during World War I virtually sealed the matter for ever.

All pictures: The Corniche brought back to Rolls-Royce all the virtues of the handcrafted coachwork on which their original reputation had been built. It is still probably the most luxuriously-appointed car available anywhere in the world.

Below: A pair of almost regal stature, the Silver Spirit and Silver Spur from Rolls-Royce.

But it was still possible to have a chassis/engine combination delivered to a coachbuilder and have an individual or particular body handbuilt onto it. As the ideal of mass-production became reality, this was more and more the preserve of car-makers whose products were already exclusive – and therefore expensive. Things like the Depression reduced the demand for expensive cars and also killed off large numbers of small family concerns, which is what the coachbuilders typically were. More and more builders of what we might now term luxury limousines turned away from coachbuilding to steel bodies as time went on, partly because of the cost, partly because of a growing dearth of craftsmen with the necessary skills.

When Park Ward entered the trade – for it could now hardly be described as an industry – in the early thirties, they were thus in something of a minority. Rolls-Royce, purveyors of cars which had always been at the expensive end of a luxury market, turned to them fairly swiftly and began a lengthy association which culminated in the purchase of Park Ward by Rolls-Royce in 1939.

The Derby company had acquired Bentley from Woolf 'Babe' Barnato in 1931, and in the period leading up to World War II had more or less used Bentley as manufacturers of 'cheap' Rolls-Royce designs with bodywork instead of the customary Rolls-Royce luxury coachwork.

Even after the war the situation persisted, but the lack of craftsmen was by then almost total and Rolls-Royce themselves, through Park Ward, began to standardize on steel bodywork from 1946 onwards. The virtues of the craftsman-built car persisted, though, and continue right up to the present day. Every single Rolls-Royce leaves the factory with a dashboard painstakingly made from layers of walnut veneer glued to a hardwood base, stained to bring out the grain and varnished to a deep shine. And for each dashboard a sample of wood is retained at the factory,

with records showing the individual car to which it belongs so it can be perfectly matched if necessary.

Modern techniques later allowed the hand-rolling of steel panels to an individual shape of compound curves, which are so smooth they could pass for the product of a stamping press but are constructed with the kind of careful attention to detail that no press in the world can match. In the fifties Rolls-Royce added one of the last surviving coachbuilding companies, H J Mulliner, to their list of acquisitions, and combined the firm with their existing coachbuilding operation to create Mulliner Park Ward – although individual Rolls-Royce cars also continued to be finished by another independent survivor, James Young at Bromley.

From this setup came two more vehicles which were in every way worthy of the Rolls-Royce heritage, intended to restore the personal custombuilt feeling with which the company had started its life, and which were to be different to the 'ordinary' unitary construction Rolls-Royce cars. Unveiled in 1971, the Corniche had separate chassis and Mulliner Park Ward coachwork, and was available in two body styles, two-door sedan or convertible. The engine was a 6.75-liter item of undisclosed power, capable of propelling the car to over 120mph; it went from standstill to 80mph in 16.9 seconds. Not bad for a heavyweight which tops 5200lbs kerb weight.

Aside from coachwork and walnut veneer inside and that exquisite V8 under the hood, the Corniche was fully loaded with all the luxury options. Built into the airconditioning system were both inside and outside temperature sensors; once the desired heat is dialed up inside the car – on the day it is delivered - it need never be altered. Even on the convertible, the outside sensor reacts to drops in outside temperature by turning the heating up to match.

Building on the success of the Corniche came what is still the most expensive production car in the world, at more than $100,000 in ex-factory trim. Introduced in

Above and right: The Rolls-Royce Camargue is the current 'top of the range' model, although it's hard to imagine any of the current Crewe-built cars being anything but.

Below: The Silver Spirit is the Rolls-Royce 'base' model.

1975, the new Rolls-Royce Camargue was styled by Pininfarina, its coachwork was by Mulliner Park Ward, the floorpan was ex-Silver Shadow, and the powerplant was the same trusted 6.75-liter V8, which on this slightly lighter (only 51,351lb) two-door is good for 115mph.

Brakes on the entire range of Rolls-Royce cars are not dual circuit, they're triple circuit. And they are now disk brakes, although Rolls-Royce were probably the last car manufacturer in the world to adopt the system, partly because there was nothing wrong with their existing massive drum brakes and partly because they refused to accept the squealing noises to which early disk brakes were susceptible. When, and *only* when, that had been successfully dealt with, disk brakes – silent disk brakes – became standard on their cars. If you've just spent $100,000 you want to *hear* that clock – except even that's been silenced by electronics.

Below: The first word in excellence and the last word in luxury – the outstanding Rolls-Royce Camargue.

Shelby Cobra

Above: There are few superlatives which cannot be used in connection with Carroll Shelby's Cobra. Those which cannot are generally connected with creature comforts. This is a 289 version from 1965.

Texan Carroll Hall Shelby turned to the manufacture of race cars at the beginning of the sixties. Before that he had been a notable race driver, had driven the neat little Spyder for Porsche, won the 1959 Le Mans 24 Hours for Aston Martin and was intimately familiar with the subtleties of race-car design and development. He was also familiar with the way European-built road cars outhandled practically anything built in the United States, although they were unable to get near the big V8s when it came to sheer power. Shelby developed the idea to combine the best of both worlds, matching an agile European chassis and suspension with an American V8. He turned to AC Cars at Thames Ditton, England, for the chassis, while the body was an extremely basic piece of folded sheet metal to form an open two-seater with a very long hood and a tiny cramped driver's cockpit perched in front of a short, bobbed deck.

Shelby's engines came from Ford. His proposition came at exactly the right moment, as Lee Iacocca was putting together the Total Performance Program. And they were planning to build their own sportscar anyway – the Mustang was due out in 1965. Better still, since Shelby was well aware that building race cars was not a sound financial proposition, his car was designed to be a street car as well. The prototype was built in the

Below: Only the blue GT500 is as it came from the factory; both its companions have been customized in some way. However the Shelby Mustangs have a brute appeal all their own, and must rank among the most awesome street cars produced during the sixties' musclecar era.

Above: The 289 Cobra ready to race, although it's unlikely that this pristine 1965 version will be subjected to it.

Left: Even in street trim, the Cobra's appointments could hardly be described as luxurious, and there are some who would dispute the use of the word 'adequate.'

In 1965 the Cobras brought Ford (and the United States) its first World Manufacturers' Championship, finally realizing Shelby's ambition to 'blow Ferrari's ass off.' To win the title his Cobras had done exactly that at Daytona, Sebring, Oulton Park, Nürburgring, Rossfeld, Rheims and, the ultimate insult, Monza – Ferrari's home territory. The only reverse was at Le Mans, when the Cobras ran second to Ferrari. Shelby could probably have cracked even that had he used the big 7-liter engines, but quite apart from getting the tiny Cobras to handle an engine easily capable of giving them a top end well in excess of 250mph, Shelby was dubious about offending Ford, whose infant GT (later the GT 40) was already competing in that class and not doing terribly well.

At the dragstrip the Cobra was so invincible that eventually the rules were changed to keep it out, but privateer Cobras continue to hand out defeat to the also-rans on every oval racetrack in America. In November 1965 Craig Breedlove took a Cobra to Bonneville and grabbed 23 national and international records. Then there were the streetgoing Cobras, which have been a sportscar high-water mark ever since they were first built. Since the first one left the factory premises the Cobra is the car to which all aspiring sportscars must be compared, and all have been found to be lacking.

Eventually the 427ci engine Ford introduced in 1963 found its way under the Cobra hood and immediately gave snakebite new fangs. Out of the 1011 Cobras built by Shelby only 356 were these real scorchers. The 427, coil-sprung, alloy-bodied Cobras had a performance curve which was as good as vertical, going straight up like something out of the Apollo space program. A massive 485hp meant that the 427 was capable of an incredible 0-60 time of 4.3 seconds, although some versions could do it in 3.8. The 0-100 time was 8.6 seconds, 0-100 and stop again was managed in 14 seconds, standing quarters vanished in 12.2 seconds, and it had a top speed of 162mph.

The press were understandably enthusiastic: 'it's only fair to warn you that out of the 300 guys who switched to the 427 Cobra only two went back to women...' was one comment.

In 1965, with the FIA GT Championship under his belt, Shelby withdrew the Cobras from competition. They were succeeded on the track by the Ford GT, but the project produced little in the way of results until it was passed over to Shelby. The car immediately and repeatedly fulfilled Shelby's dream, leaving the red Ferraris in their dust as they won the 24 Heures du Mans in 1966, 1967, 1968 and 1969.

But Ford were committed to Total Performance mainly as a sales tool, believing strongly in the adage 'race on Sunday, sell on Monday.' In 1967 Cobra production ended because Ford wanted to concentrate on the GT cars since they were still a major boost to Mustang sales, while the Cobra had no production-line counterpart at Dearborn.

But word was already out that there would soon be a Federal ban on horsepower advertising, and an assortment of other regulations designed to remove performance cars from the streets. Soon Shelby asked Ford president Lee Iacocca to release him from the Total Performance Program and the days of legend were ended, although the Cobra now survives in more replica variants than possibly any other single automobile. However desirable those may be, current owners of the genuine article will already be aware of what Ford found out all those years ago: there's nothing like the real thing, and the Cobra was it.

workshop Shelby shared with drag racer Dean Moon, and used the new 221ci smallblock V8.

Despite Shelby's apparent concessions to Ford's cost accountants, mass production was something never destined to be part of the Cobra story; each and every car was lovingly handbuilt and as improvements were made to the breed they were simply built into the next car along the line, so there are virtually no two Cobras the same. Furthermore, as the improvements became common knowledge many owners brought their cars back to the works to have them brought up to date. So although the first 75 Cobras were fitted with the 221 V8 bored out to 260ci, when Ford offered the engine as a 289 in their own lineup and Shelby adopted it, many of the existing Cobra owners brought their earlier cars back for a transplant.

It wasn't until 1962 that the Cobra was first let loose on a racetrack; at Riverside that October Billy Krause built up a lead of a mile and a half over the rest of the field before breaking a stub axle on his red 289. It was an unhappy reason for retirement, but the potential of the car had been clearly established and over the next three years every race driver in America was faced with a simple choice: either experience snakebite – or suffer from it.

Stutz

Based on New York's Fifth Avenue, the re-emergent Stutz company are currently reviving what was probably the best-known name in the American auto industry during the twenties. Rather than a replica or a nostalgic copycat design, they are attempting what is potentially the most difficult task in this area. Chrysler stylist Virgil Exner, responsible for so many of those stunning show cars, has combined original body parts with a current design to create the flavour of the prewar era with modern looks and running gear.

Built in Modena by Carrozzeria Padana, the Black Hawk features a squared-off radiator shell, curving fenders and external, chromed exhausts which are more reminiscent of the hotrodders' lakes pipes than the convoluted chrome headers of the thirties. Powered by a selection of GM V8 units according to customer choice, the Black Hawk, at more than 5000lbs, is a heavyweight with a matching sticker price. It is also pretentiously ugly, though built to high standards.

In fact, in many respects the modern Black Hawk is a fairly good counterpart to the earlier models, at least in appearance. But not only were they somewhat stubby in looks, they were also rather coarse, even brutish to drive, and owners of their only serious homegrown rivals coined the insult 'you have to be nuts to drive a Stutz.' By way of retaliation the Stutz owners made up their own verse: 'there never was a worser car than a Mercer.' In truth the Mercer fans had something of a point, since the Mercer Raceabout was unquestionably a far handier car than the big Stutz. However the extra power paid off and Stutz won more races than Mercer.

Indeed it was the Stutz Black Hawk which came so close to ending the domination of Le Mans by W O's Bentley Boys, splitting the pack neatly in 1928. Had it not been for a lost top gear at 2.30pm, just 90 minutes before the end of the race, the Stutz may have done better than second place. As it was, 'Babe' Barnato managed to hang onto his lead, but the crippled Black Hawk still came home ahead of the other two 4.5-liter Bentleys. It was then the best placing for an American car in the event, and would remain so for another 38 years until the string of victories which Ford's GT 40 began from 1966 onward.

Harry C Stutz built his first car – actually a gas buggy – in 1897. In 1905 he produced the American Underslung which, as its name suggests, had its chassis slung beneath the springs in an attempt to lower the center of gravity. Although it was probably not the best solution to the problem, Stutz continued his pursuit of the right answer, and it was a low frame allowing high cornering speeds that enabled the Black Hawk to give the Bentleys such a hard time at Le Mans.

Stutz had begun as a maker of motor parts, and it was the need to demonstrate the ruggedness of his rear axle

Below: The Stutz Black Hawk sedan of 1929, and (*right*) engine detail of the same car.

which prompted him to enter the very first Indianapolis 500 in 1911. The car ran faultlessly and finished eleventh, which was a tribute to the axle and also to a variety of other makers' parts.

Stutz at the time was building what were called 'assembled' cars: like many others they made some parts themselves and bought the rest in. The engines were initially Wisconsin T-heads, although by 1913 they had been dropped in favour of four and six-cylinder Stutz engines. With these Stutz came third at the 1913 Indy, a better result and a better advert.

1914 saw the advent of the Stutz Bearcat, a 6.5-liter four-cylinder T-head of some 60hp which was developed at 1500rpm, and it was this car which prompted the great rivalry between Stutz and Mercer owners. In 1915 the first Stutz racing team appeared. Known as the 'White Squadron' thanks to their all-white livery and racing coveralls, they were placed third, fourth and seventh at Indy and won a selection of other events across America.

Then in 1916 a disgruntled Bearcat owner took his car back to a dealer and complained that smaller-engined Mercers were beating him. Although there were few, if any, roads, this so-called 'lemon' was passed to 'Cannonball' Baker for a massively-publicised attempt on the coast-to-coast record, then held by a motorcycle. Both the Bearcat and its driver created a legend – since infrequently and illegally revived by Brock Yates – as 'Cannonball' scorched across the American heartland in 11 days, seven and a half hours, breaking only a shock-absorber clip along the way.

In 1919 Harry Stutz parted from the company which bore his name, going on to build an unsuccessful vehicle called the HCS. After an uninspiring period under the control of Charles Schwab, Stutz was taken over by Frederick Moscovics, whose stated intention was a concentration on 'safety, beauty and comfort.' The first car produced under his rule was thus a four-seat tourer known as the Safety Stutz, a straight eight of 4.7 liters with a chain-driven overhead camshaft, giving 92hp at 3200rpm. The chassis was a low-slung device whose small ground clearance was partly the benefit produced by the use of a worm-drive rear axle. The brakes were quite literally hydraulic, using water and alcohol-filled bags to press the brake shoes up against the drums.

On the same chassis came a two-seater Black Hawk, based on Frank Lockhart's 3-liter land speed record car which Stutz had built and which had taken the American Class D record at 198mph. It was a version of this which did so well in the 1928 24 Hours at Le Mans, although in 1929 it could only manage fifth place. For 1930 the Black Hawk was improved, growing to 5.25 liters and switching to Lockheed hydraulic brakes. It is said that 24 blown Black Hawks were built to take on the Bentleys at Le Mans, but apparently none have survived – if indeed they were ever built.

The following year the extra power needed to make the cars competitive was achieved by the use of new cylinder heads. This dual ohc engine was known as the DV 32, had four valves per cylinder and was fitted to a variety of different models, including the new Bearcat Torpedo Speedster and the 1933 Super Bearcat.

This rather stumpy-looking two-seat ragtop was virtually the end of the line for Stutz, and by 1935 they had stopped making cars altogether. It would be more than 20 years before the United States produced anything else which could genuinely be described as a sportscar. That too made its debut in New York, at the 1953 Autorama. A white two-seater, the GM executives had named it Corvette.

Below: A 1929 Stutz Model M Dual Cowl Phaeton, currently on display in the ACD Museum.

740

Talbot Lago

The Sunbeam-Talbot-Darracq combine of 1919 was ambitious if unsuccessful. Talbot had been formed originally with the backing of Lord Shrewsbury and Talbot to build the cars of Frenchman Adolphe Clément in Britain.

The first cars were originally called Clément-Talbots, but the name was later simplified to Talbot. Alexandre Darracq had made his fortune from bicycles and built his first car in 1902, a two-cylinder device which was immortalized as *Genevieve* in the film of the same name. After a variety of successful cars had been built Darracq retired in 1913, leaving the company to continue under different management. French de-

signer Louis Coatelen had begun work with Humber in 1901, moved from there to Hillman and then on to Sunbeam where he was responsible for the successful series of Sunbeam race cars which were prominent just before the outbreak of World War I and again in the twenties, by which time he was designing for STD. In 1934 the STD combine, with the fine reputation gained by the racing Talbots built at the Suresnes factory earning them the nickname 'the invincibles,' was broken up, all the British assets going to the Rootes group along with the Sunbeam and Talbot names. Anthony Lago took over the French assets and the Talbot-Darracq name, although the French tax laws

Left: The 1949 Talbot Lago Grandsport, as first campaigned at Le Mans.

Below: Prewar Talbots had earned the company a good reputation. This 1933 Roesch Talbot 90 was bodied in Britain by Vanden Plas.

were slowly forcing the demise of firms like Talbot, Hotchkiss and Delahaye.

But the Talbot continued to race, and it was a prewar Lago SS chassis which formed the basis for their legendary Le Mans racer of the late forties and early fifties, the Lago Grandsport. The car was a strange beast for a serious Le Mans racer, being drastically underpowered but thus reliable and economical – ideally suited for long-distance endurance racing. In fact the same car was entered for Le Mans in private hands five times between 1949 and 1953 by André Chambas and finished the punishing event on all but one occasion.

Below: The side view of this 1948 Talbot Lago Grandsport shows its long hood, economical lines and streamlined appearance very clearly indeed.

The wheelbase was 104 inches, front suspension was independent and at the rear the chassis rails ran beneath the live axle which had semi-elliptic springs. The engine was a 4.4-liter straight six which had been introduced on the 1946 Lago Record, when it had delivered 170hp. For 1948 the power was upped to 190hp by the use of three Zenith carburetors. All the cars were fitted with a Wilson preselector gearbox, and were commonly sold as a bare chassis; bodywork for the Lago was variable according to taste and many attractive examples were the product of Figoni, Chapron or Saoutchik.

Works Talbot racers wore completely open light-weight two-seater bodywork, in which they were regularly campaigned at Le Mans. However it was those races between 1949 and 1953 which were so successfully campaigned by the private Lago which tend to catch the imagination and stick in the memory. André Chambas bodied his car with a closed coupé-style affair which featured a shed-like cutoff tail with a near-vertical rear window slit. The flat hood and curved, streamlined front end are typical of the period and drew heavily on the styles which were current among the famous names of the time.

In its first race, in 1949, Chambas shared his drive with veteran *pilote* André Morel, who was then nearly 60 years old and had a vast experience of racing to draw on. Much of it was with Lagos and he was, happily, a product controller at the Talbot factory. So although the privateer entrant was never works-supported, his car was checked over by works mechanics prior to each visit to the Sarthe circuit.

The first outing had mixed results, as the car ran out of fuel on the mandatory winding-down lap and was credited with running for only 23 hours and 59 minutes, having completed 1861 miles in that time. However it had survived in all but bureaucratic name, and had done a great deal better than the official works team since none of their cars completed the distance.

In 1950 the works cars established a strong lead and a brand-new Lago driven by Rosier (*père et fils*) came in first with their previous year's mount following them home under the guidance of Meyrat and Mairesse. André Chambas, with team-mate André Morel, also finished, in a creditable thirteenth place. This year they had covered 1915 miles at an average of 79mph.

For the following year Chambas followed the example of the works team, placing his coupé body into careful storage and replacing it with an open aluminum two-seater. Although similar in design, this featured a full-fendered body rather than the cycle fenders fitted to the works cars. While the new body was noticeably lighter the car did slightly worse at Le Mans, covering a shorter distance and averaging a slower speed for the 24 hours. The race was won by Jaguar, with the only survivor of the three works-entered Lagos (of Meyrat and Mairesse) finishing second; privateers Levegh and Marchand finished fourth in their Lago.

More development followed, and in 1952 the redoubtable Chambas and his car reappeared at the Sarthe circuit sporting dual roots-type blowers and two big Zenith carburetors. With a low (6:1) compression ratio the Lago's stock 190hp was boosted to 235hp, which gave the car a top speed of around 140mph on the long Mulsanne Straight. Even with this extra loading, the mighty six-cylinder engine ran with supreme reliability as the works cars dropped out one by one. At the end of the 24 hours the Lago of Chambas and Morel was the last remaining Talbot and finished the event a very good ninth.

It must be remembered that the early fifties were the days of the big battles between the works teams of Mercedes and Jaguar, with Porsche *et al* just beginning to raise their heads and their sights; the old, prewar Le Mans of the privateer was succumbing swiftly to the megabuck professionalism of the factories and anyone who did well as a private entrant had achieved something to be proud of.

1953 was to be the last outing for the Chambas Lago;

Morel retired at the end of 1952 and was replaced by another experienced racer named de Cortanze. More work on the supercharging, plus replacing the Zeniths with Solex carbs, had given another 5-10hp, but the works teams were making upwards of 160mph on the Mulsanne; trying to keep up, Chambas spun at Tertre Rouge and, reversing to clear the track, overheated the friction bands in the preselector gearbox and could no longer select any forward gears, ending both his race and the racing career of the car.

The coupé body was replaced after the race and superchargers were removed, the engine being restored to stock. Sold in 1957, the car went first to America, then to Switzerland and is now in the hands of a private collector in Britain, where it makes occasional forays to events for historic marques.

Below: By 1959 the Grandsport had given way to this 2.5-liter Talbot Lago America, with more than just the red paintwork evoking the feel of contemporary Ferraris.

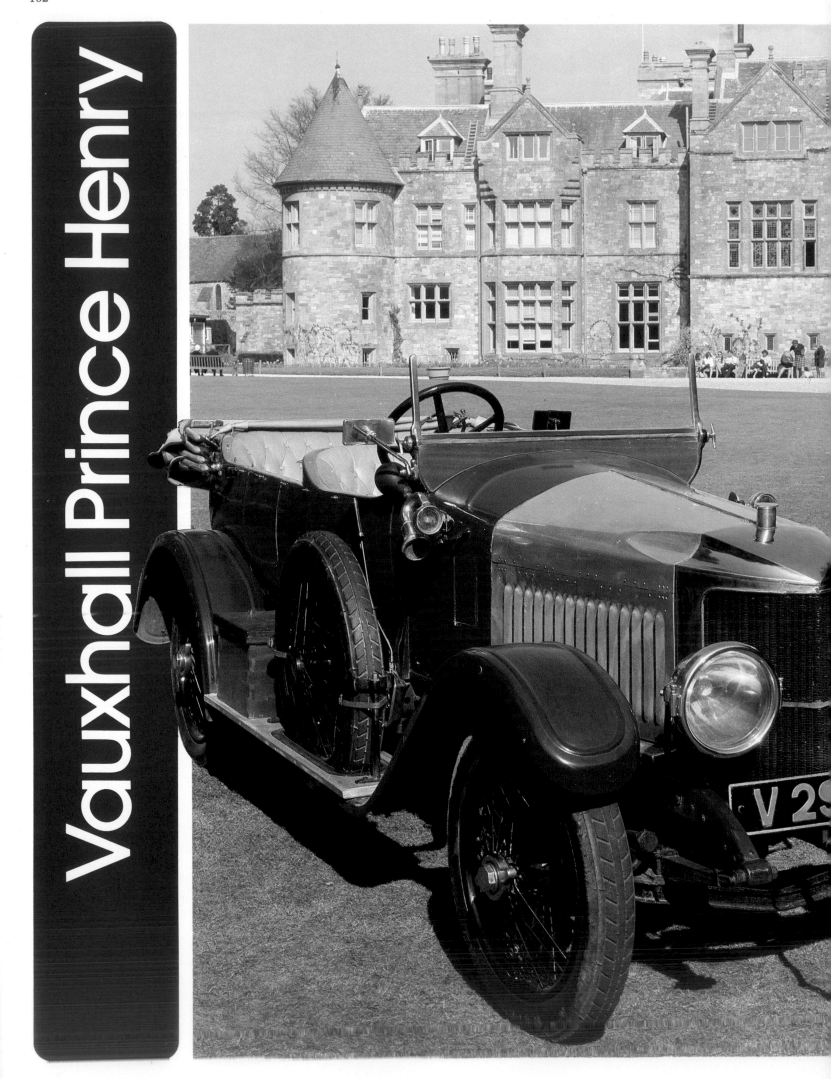

Vauxhall Prince Henry

Above: Vauxhall's griffon emblem was adopted at the company's formation and remains so today. It has been identified with the site at London's Vaux Hall (where the cars were first built) since the days of the Norman conquest.

Left: The beginnings of the hood flutes which characterized Vauxhall cars for about 50 years can be seen on this 1914 model.

Below: A 1922 trials specification Vauxhall based on a Prince Henry chassis.

The Vauxhall Iron Works had been making marine engines at their premises in London's Wandsworth Road – in the Vauxhall area – since 1857, when the company was founded by Scotsman Alexander Wilson. In 1903 R W Hodges and J H Chambers built their first single-cylinder passenger car and in 1906 moved to Luton to concentrate on the manufacture of cars in earnest. From their earliest beginnings their interest in motorsport was intense, and the company began to forge a reputation for itself in various kinds of trials, sprints and races.

At the time one of the major events on the international sporting calendar was the International Touring Car Competition for the Herkomer Trophy which started from Frankfurt, ran a 500-mile road course to Innsbruck and finished with a hillclimb at Semmering and then a very brief speed trial. Begun by a portrait painter, Professor Hubert von Herkomer, in 1905, it was intended for heavy touring cars in stock condition, although a rule change from 1906 meant that there were, from then on, some very lightweight bodies paying only token service to the heavy tourer designation formerly stipulated.

One of the most enthusiastic Herkomer competitors was Prince Henry of Prussia, younger brother to the Kaiser, and when the Herkomer event ended after only three years Prince Henry launched his own. It too was meant for full four-seater touring cars, and there was a bore restriction of 146mm for four-cylinder engines and 120mm for six-cylinders. Although 'trade entrants,' meaning professional or semi-professional works teams, were barred, there were a number of recognized drivers in some fairly exotic machines. This first event under the new name was won by Fritz Erle in a 50hp Benz, which set what would become the recognized standard for sportscars from then on, with flaring full fenders and streamlined front valance rising over the suspension into the radiator grille.

The 1910 event included no particularly noteworthy vehicles, but 1911 saw the début of two cars which were named after it; the winning Austro-Daimler Prinz Heinrich (designed and driven by Ferdinand Porsche), and the Vauxhall Prince Henry.

Laurence Pomeroy, who came to Vauxhall in 1907, was the designer who took the company into competitive motorsport from 1908 onwards when he managed to boost the output of the rather staid four-cylinder 20hp model up to a more-than-respectable 40-plus hp;

it was this high-output engine which was installed in a team of three cars entered for the 1910 Prince Henry event. The bodies for the mandatory four-seat tourer were of lightweight construction – there were, for example, no doors – and the radiator ended in a sharp point. The radiator shell was fluted at the top, and the scallops were extended along the line of the louvered hood; the scalloped hood was to be a feature of Vauxhall design right up to the fifties and early sixties.

Although the cars had a respectable top speed of around 75mph, they failed to distinguish themselves by winning the event. They were among the first of the purpose-built sportscars, however, even though the term had yet to be coined at the time they were made, and their ride and handling combination was directed to precisely this end. This meant that they were not among the most comfortable cars in which to travel long distances, but the engines were both flexible and sturdy, gaining a solid reputation for smooth running.

Inevitably the car went into production after the event, even though its appointments were somewhat basic. After a while doors were added as a concession to those who wished to carry passengers or travel in reasonable style. Later still, in 1913, the engine was enlarged to four liters, giving a small improvement to

Far left: Last of the Prince Henrys, a 1925 model.

Left: Cockpit detail from a 1923 30/98 and (*right*) the engine of the same car.

Below: A 1924 30/98 tourer, with four doors.

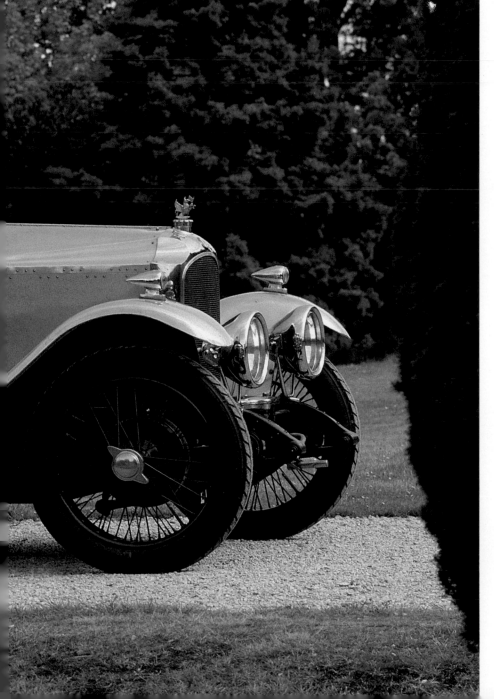

top speed but most significantly providing a much greater amount of low-end torque and thus the sort of pulling-power a genuine four-seat touring car might regularly need.

With the bigger engine came much more solid bodies and a general all-round refinement: some cars were even fitted with a closed coupé body. These bigger and more solid cars were far more popular than the original lightweights, a fact evident from the much higher numbers of later models which survive today. There is a two-seat Prince Henry at the National Motor Museum in Beaulieu, England, and one of the earlier models take pride of place in Vauxhall's own museum.

The Prince Henry was further developed as the Vauxhall 30/98, and it is this model which many regard as being the true Vauxhall classic of the period. In original form it was built for hillclimbing for one Joseph Higginson and from this it became a somewhat heavyweight tourer. It was officially described as a sports tourer, and perhaps might have enjoyed better success than its illustrious forebear had not its namesake's brother plunged Europe into war when he did. In any case, with 4.5 liters and most of its available power coming in as solid low-end punch, it clattered and roared its way into the hearts of contemporary (and much more modern) enthusiasts.

Emerging from the gloom of the immediate postwar period, Vauxhall continued their role as manufacturers of large cars with that same 30/98. The first RAC Tourist Trophy after the war was held at the Isle of Man in 1922 and for this event the RAC applied 1921 rules about engine capacity though everyone else had lowered to just two liters for the 1922 season. The 1922 TT was for three-liter cars, though, with the result that only nine cars – all British – were entered, and Vauxhall went to the great expense of preparing a team of three cars based around the three-liter 30/98, using a dohc layout which was rendered obsolete for racing purposes the minute the wet and misty event was over. Small wonder that 1922 was the last year in which Vauxhall themselves took an active part in motor racing.

In 1925, just as the company were launching a new model with single-sleeve valves and getting gradually into financial difficulties, they were taken over by General Motors and from then on increasingly toed a company line which was firm but benevolent. When the German Opel company was also gathered into the GM fold there was an increasing amount of crosstalk between the two companies, and the individuality which produced such cars as the Prince Henry and 30/98 was gone forever.

Hotrodding is traditionally believed to have begun in California and spread across the United States from there. It was brought to England in the very early seventies as a deliberate cultural import, and embracing it completely required a conscious attempt at adopting a foreign lifestyle and attitudes, even if it was only at weekends.

Because of this, hotrodding caught on slowly in Britain. With no lack of enthusiasm, there was a distinct shortage of information and an even greater shortage of suitable hardware. One of the first people to produce something which was hailed at the time as having a genuinely authentic appearance was Nick Butler, who spent 2500 hours building *Nykilodeon*, a bucket T in the finest traditions, powered by a 371 Olds V8 engine.

It featured a large number of things which would

soon become commonplace on British street rods, borrowed heavily from racetrack experience and even included a brake compensator which came directly from a Brabham race car. The economy of design which racetrack necessity dictates clearly appealed to Butler, and it was not to be the last time that he would borrow from the Formula One circus.

First, however, he followed *Nykilodeon* with *Revenge*, a blistering C-cab which included a number of novel features and established Butler as a major force in streetrodding in the UK – so major that he was one of the first to make it his business, setting up Auto Imagination to design and build anything involved with cars. His brass-spoke steering wheels and brass Model T radiators became standard equipment on most of the Model Ts built in Britain. His engineering parts were everywhere, made to measure or off the

shelf. *Revenge* was followed by *Andromeda*, another blown T, this time for a customer and carrying a fairly impressive pricetag.

The follow-up was planned to be something extra special. Built in conjunction with Wolfrace Wheels, the project was eventually to be called *Sonic* – named after one of the Wolfrace wheel ranges – and was intended to be a sportscar with two of everything, including engines. Most of the problems seemed to be fairly straightforward and multiple engines had been used successfully before in a number of applications. But using a pair of V8 engines in a street car presented some new challenges.

Placing the engines side by side meant that the installation wouldn't be too wide and that they could each feed drive to the rear axle directly. Longitudinal placement would have meant linking the engines

Above: Sonic, designed and built by Nick Butler for Wolfrace Wheels, as it appeared originally in blue, and (*left*) since its new coloring was added.

directly or facing up to insuperable driveline problems. With two differentials in the independent rear axle, the problems would be soaked up.

But giving two independent power sources the unitary smoothness and tractability demanded in a road car was still a headache. Combining the activities of two separate automatic transmissions served only to complicate the situation even further.

The solution, when it came, was not a mechanical or simple engineering answer and led Auto Imagination into a new field which was at the time occupying the attentions of all the world's major auto manufacturers: the micro-electronics of the onboard computer. But for *Sonic* it had to be a great deal more than something which calculated time, distance and fuel consumption, more than a computer which metered fuel and apportioned high-voltage electricity across a carefully-determined advance curve.

The computer has the use of 100 inputs and 100 outputs; the startup procedure alone requires 80 pieces of information going in and 90 going out. The engines are started individually, and the computer allows the selection of any idle speed up to 3000rpm on each engine. Once they're both fired up, the 'synch' control on the pushbutton dash hands engine balancing over to the computer and the two V8s work in perfect harmony. If either powerplant goes out of sync by more than 500rpm or for longer than eight seconds the computer automatically cuts the throttles back to idling speed.

Although if one engine cuts out the computer will allow the journey to continue on the other alone, it still shows the traditional failings of all computers in that it is incapable of reasoning or allowing for non-program events. For example, when the propshaft sensor, which monitors rotation of the shaft and thus computes rpm for the tachometer, was broken by some piece of road debris, the computer reacted in typical fashion. Getting high throttle input but no rpm it deduced malfunction and shut down.

Failsafe devices are infinitely preferable to the other alternatives, however frustrating they might be at times. The automatic transmission is pushbutton-operated, but selection of park or reverse requires the simultaneous pressing of two separate buttons to ensure that it can't be done by accident.

As a final failsafe, there are ventilated disk brakes all round, using four-pot floating calipers at the front. The setup is the same as Tyrrell used on their six-wheel Formula One car, and can be considered well proven.

The end result is a car which, although driveable, is not perhaps entirely practical thanks to a complete lack of weather protection and a certain parking-lot vulnerability. Nevertheless the car, which has already changed from its original color to the deep maroon in which it appeared at the British Grand Prix in 1984, does see road use for promotional events.

In that respect, then, it is perfectly qualified to be considered a true dream car, being visionary, rare, expensive and – occasionally – driveable.

Although it looks as if it was built for a science-fiction movie, *Sonic* (*left and below*) was in fact built to be driven. It incorporates a great deal of microchip technology which has yet to find its way onto the production lines of those large auto builders who have been investing millions in research for several decades.

Index

Page numbers in italics refer to illustrations